I0554849

the Sleeping Ute

ROBERT OLIVER BROWN

BLUEPRINT PRESS
INTERNATIONALE

The Sleeping Ute
Copyright © 2023 by Robert Oliver Brown

All rights reserved. No part of this publication may be reproduced, distributed, or transmitted in any form or by any means, including photocopying, recording, or other electronic or mechanical methods, without the prior written permission of the author, except in the case of brief quotations embodied in critical reviews and certain other non-commercial uses permitted by copyright law.

ISBN
978-1-959365-81-5 (Paperback)
978-1-959365-82-2 (eBook)
978-1-959365-80-8 (Hardcover)

Table of Contents

A SACRED PRAYER

O' Great Spirit, I seek strength,
not to be greater than my brother,
but to fight my greatest enemy, myself.
Make me always ready to come to you
with clean hands and straight eyes,
so, when life fades, as the fading sunset,
my spirit may come to you without shame.

—–Chief Yellow Lark—–

ACKNOWLEDGEMENTS

I wish to thank my wife for setting a high example and for standing by and supporting me in the journeys I have taken thus far in life. Her example has aided me in my search to discover more about my true selfhood.

I also wish to thank my children, for keeping me grounded and patient. There is no greater honor than the responsibility of raising a family.

Finally, I would like to express my gratitude to the American Indians living on reservations.

AUTHOR'S LITERARY DISCLAIMER

This book is a work of fiction based upon real life events. It presents a fictionalized portrayal of the Ute Mountain Ute Tribe and their governmental operations. Any resemblance to individuals or locations is purely coincidental.

PRELUDE

All life in this phase of existence is one grand adventure: an adventure in which we grow spiritually and in our understanding.

Finding one's purpose and reason for being remains one of the greatest mysteries in this brief journey we call life. Our time here should go beyond becoming an adult, having a job, getting married, starting a family, saying farewell to loved ones along the way, and eventually dying. One's purpose should be to advance one's understanding about their Creator, their fellowmen, and themself.

My main mission in writing this book is to introduce some thoughts and ideas which might act as a spiritual awakening and help you view others with more love and be more considerate of their feelings and beliefs.

* * * * *

PROLOGUE

Long before our forefathers arrived on this side of the earth, North America was populated with various tribes of indigenous people who had simple and peaceful lives. They lived for generations respecting the Earth, caring for and nurturing her.

Their aim in life was not to amass wealth or own materialistic possessions. Instead, it was to live peacefully with all of God's creations, including animals. Killing was only done for survival and out of need, never for sport.

One might think we are better off now because our forefathers helped bring about the greatest scientific and cultural changes in history. One might say that without such "progress", the American Indians might even still be living in teepees.

On the other hand, one might question if we really are better off. After all, we have created weapons which could destroy humanity, and forever alter the face of the earth. We have changed the courses of rivers and dammed up large bodies of water and waged war upon our own environment, endangering humans and animals alike.

Over time, humankind has slipped away from the spiritual aspects concerning life and stopped relying on inner feelings. Instead, we rely on our human logic. Great physical healing through spiritual reasoning and prayer is just now being reintroduced.

As you read through the following pages, you will find me using "God", the Christian name to describe the Divine power. But this book is for everyone who believes in a higher power, whether they call that power God, the Great Spirit, Jehovah, Allah, or the many other names the people of the world use to pray, worship, and celebrate the divine power of their faith. And, while the names vary, many of the faiths of the world share two fundamental truths. A strong belief in power higher than themselves. And a belief in a hereafter, a place of existence beyond our physical realm.

Just as importantly, this book is for those who struggle with faith, or even doubt the existence of a higher power. Perhaps their battles have been too difficult and their challenges to unsurmountable to believe in a divine power they feel has abandoned them.

Wherever your heart lies at this moment, it is my sincere hope that once you put this book down, you take away a sense of hope. Or, at the very least a sense of curiosity and perhaps interest in finding your own connection to a higher power, one that inspires you and fills you with a sense of purpose.

I invite you to share my latest adventure and the revelations I discovered from a Ute Indian elder and holy man in Towaoc, Colorado. On our journey it is my hope you will discover unknowns and mysteries about others and yourself — discoveries that will enable you to rise higher in your understanding of life and even into boundless bliss and happiness. We will learn that our fears and misconceptions of life and of our fellowmen exist only in our minds and are waiting to be discovered and realized, so they can fade away and be replaced by enlightenment.

* * * * *

Chapter 1

"The Awakening"

My story begins at a time in my life when I felt like I was being prepared to make this journey. A time when I was contemplating not only a career change, but a shift in my mindset. A change that eventually led me to Jake, an Ute holy man in Towaoc, Colorado. And, to my destiny.

* * * * *

After serving in the United States Army in Berlin, Germany, in the late fifties, I returned to Wichita, Kansas where I grew up with a broader understanding and compassion for people. I served in Berlin after the Berlin Airlift, before the shameful Berlin wall was ever built. Berlin was divided into four sectors: American, Russian, British, and French.

Shortly after returning home, I reunited with my high school sweetheart, Belinda Joneson. I also started a career in aviation at the Boeing Company in Wichita. It was a career that would last for twelve years. Shortly after starting with the Boeing Company, I married Belinda. After three years of marriage, we purchased a home and started our family. We had a son, Jason, and a daughter, Renee. I became content at this point with my job and comfortable lifestyle.

Put another way; I became content with pursuing and living the American Dream. I'm sure many of my fellow Americans were pursuing the same dream. We were all raising our children, trying to instill in them the same values and goals our parents had instilled in us which their parents had instilled in them. And like my parents I purchased a home, worked an eight-hour day, five days a week, attended a church, was active in the local parent-teacher association where my children attended school, joined one of the major political parties, took a two-week family vacation each year, and strived to save money for my children's education. I'm not saying this was a bad course, but as I looked around, it was the same course the mainstream was on.

At this point, I questioned how this pre-designed course had been and instilled in so many. I suppose it was a way to keep people busy and in line with society's rules. Most certainly, those who adhered to this idea of being, would not become idle and bored and try to take advantage of others or the system and violate our laws.

Looking back now, I was quite content with this way of life. I was indeed living the American Dream. I believed that if I continued to work hard and not violate or break any laws, I might eventually be promoted. I could obtain a higher and more prestigious position and receive a higher salary. I might extend my vacation plans from Colorado to Europe and other exotic places.

I began to feel that this dream was unconsciously controlling my family and everyone I knew. We were all becoming a part of a very large industrial movement. This was the "power structure" many of us at that point in time had a hand in creating. This giant entity had become a way to control the masses in the world. America the Beautiful had become Corporate America. We had allowed our lives to be regulated through economic manipulation and a sense of competition to acquire more and more material possessions.

Occasionally, during a work break at the Boeing Company, I would allow my thoughts to wander, reflecting on what might be happening in my life. I began to see that if I continued the mainstream course I was on, I could predict my entire life, barring any sickness or accidents.

It was almost as if we were all on a conveyor belt from start to finish. Most of us would experience the same ride. Some of us would gain more fame and wealth than others, experiencing a smoother ride. On the other hand, some of us might endure sickness and poverty, thereby experiencing a rougher ride. Some of us might even fall off along the way due to accidents or an unfortunate turn of events.

However, one thing is certain; we will eventually all reach the end and experience death.

Realizing the course I was on and where I was headed on this conveyer belt of life, I had to stop and question if this was really all I wanted out of life. Did I want fame or fortune? What kind of legacy did I want to leave? A legacy of fame and fortune? Or a legacy that had more meaning. After looking at my options, I considered charting a new course. There had to be more to my life than a predictable ride.

I decided I was ready to jump ship. This mainstream current I was caught up in was controlling my life and every decision. This was certainly an awakening. Something within me was prompting these new feelings. Whatever this new force was, I decided to let go of all my preconceived beliefs and convictions concerning life and rely on these new feelings. I had no idea what new avenues I would follow, but I decided to turn my mind to this new force within.

One evening shortly after I came to this conclusion to break away from my safe course, I was visiting with my wife. Out of nowhere, she asked about the line of work I did while serving in the Army. I explained that aptitude tests are given to determine what you might be best suited for. Based on my test, they sent me to an academy where I trained to become a military police officer. I asked my wife why that was of interest to her. She replied that she had read in the local paper that morning that the City of Wichita was looking to hire twelve new police officers, and they were taking applications for recruits now.

This came as a complete surprise. I had not mentioned my feelings to my wife about considering a change in my line of work. I figured maybe she was being influenced by the same power that was guiding me to pursue a new path in life.

I had never really considered doing anything like law enforcement again after the Army. However, I felt compelled to read the article my wife spoke about. After reading it, I learned I had all the desired qualifications. I told Belinda I was going to pursue this opportunity. I felt an inner peace about my decision.

I decided to take off work the following day and apply for one of the positions. After submitting my application, I took a series of tests.

I returned to work the next day and continued my familiar routine. I was entrusting the outcome to a power other than myself for the first time. I continued to listen for my inner thoughts and feelings to guide me. This career change meant I would have to accept a salary that was less than one-half of my present salary. From a practicality standpoint, it didn't seem prudent. However, if I were truly entrusting the outcome of this decision to a higher power, I felt everything would work out.

The following week, I was notified by the City of Wichita that I had successfully passed my tests and had been accepted as a member of the Police Department. I was asked to come in the following week to attend an orientation meeting.

At the meeting, an opportunity was presented that would allow me to continue making the same salary I had been making at Boeing. All I had to do was complete my college education in administration of justice, which was a continuation of police science studies. This almost seemed too good to be true.

Because everything had worked out, I felt validated for my decision to make a career change. For the first time I could remember, I refused to listen to my human reasoning and doubts. Instead, I entrusted this decision to a power greater than my own. Doing so had been a blessing. My income had increased, and I had an opportunity to receive a college education. I could pursue this new adventure without denying anything for my family or changing our lifestyle.

Upon graduating Rookie School, I was assigned an area of the city very similar to the area I grew up in – an area built in the 1940s to accommodate aircraft factory workers during World War II. It was primarily a low-income, blue-collar part of the city.

I grew up attending schools with interracial classrooms. I learned at an early age how to get along with all races and not only respect everyone's differences but value them. I viewed my African American, American Indian, and Hispanic classmates as simply people and friends instead of being a specific race. My early interactions with a wide variety of races positively affected the rest of my life.

This didn't mean I didn't experience my share of growing pains. As a young boy, I was very timid. After experiencing confrontations with other children my age and enduring bullying and intimidation, I learned to take good care of myself. But not through fists and violence, but through brains and communication. As a teenager and later as a young man, the most valuable thing I learned was to be respectful and considerate of other people's feelings. Looking back on my childhood and school years, I felt more than prepared for this new position I was undertaking.

In terms of my heritage and background, I felt I was as American as anyone I knew. My father was Scotch-Irish, and my mother's father was French and Cherokee Indian. His mother was Cherokee. Her name was Talulla Crow, and I met her as a young boy. My mother's mother was German and Sioux Indian. She was born on an Indian reservation near Sioux City, Iowa. One of my mother's brothers grew up on an American Indian reservation in Norman, Oklahoma.

Due to the number of industries and types of businesses in the area of the city I was assigned patrol duty, there was a high rate of burglaries. It also had more than its share of family disturbances as well as brawls at the local bars. Friday and Saturday nights had the highest number of incidents. It helped having grown up in this area.

The department's policy was to send two single-man units to the scene of a disturbance. I always tried to arrive with impartial feelings. After separating both parties, I would listen to what each person had to say, preferably in different areas of the home or out of hearing distance from each other. It was important to make everyone involved feel what they had to say was worth being heard.

I discovered that engaging in a positive manner and treating the people involved as I would like to be treated, usually resulted in a good and peaceful outcome. Of course, there would always be exceptions when I was forced to handle the situation physically, but for the most part, I was usually successful and didn't have to make many arrests.

After I had been on the job for about six months, I received a call from my detail supervisor, Sergeant Barceau asking to meet. He was one of my favorite supervisors and we had a good working relationship. Barceau was a big, muscular Italian fellow. He never hesitated to volunteer for dangerous calls or to back up other officers.

When I met Barceau, I sensed by the look on his face and the tone of his voice that he was concerned about something. He told me he was worried about me making so many disturbance calls and one in particular. I had made a disturbance call to a location where the officer making the same call before me a few weeks earlier had been beaten up by the parties at this address. As I looked back on the call, I thought it was one where I had to get physical and make an arrest, but I thought nothing of it then.

I had been making disturbance calls in my neighboring beats on my own. I had assumed that the other beat officers were busy on other calls. Looking me squarely in the eye, Barceau said he was concerned I was starting to be used as a "legal hit man." He assured me he would check with the other supervisors and dispatchers. I respected his opinion, and told him I appreciated his concern, but I felt they were doing nothing more than leveraging my background of having grown up in the area, and I wasn't concerned. This seemed to appease him. The last thing I wanted was to cause issues for my superiors.

Overall, I enjoyed my new line of work. Little did I know; however, an event was about to happen which would change my life forever. I was dispatched to a disturbance far from my assigned beat that involved a gun at the scene of an automobile accident. I would not reach the scene of this disturbance and accident. I would not recall getting the call from the dispatcher or coming to work that day. As I was en route, with my red light and siren on, I entered an intersection on the city's outskirts. A man driving a ¾ ton pickup, traveling at a high rate of speed and under the influence of alcohol, would not see my patrol car in time to stop.

The man in the pickup laid down 240 feet of skid marks before hitting me directly in the driver's door. The traffic officer who worked the accident estimated that the pickup was traveling 63 miles per hour at the point of impact. My patrol car was thrown across the intersection into a telephone pole, breaking it in two. The double-sided impact brought my patrol car together in the middle like an accordion. At the time of the accident, there was some confusion about what police car and officer were involved, as I had been sent to another officer's beat.

Sergeant Mill was one of the first to arrive, which was fortunate for me. Mill "Mike" was a big, strong guy and a trustworthy and good friend. When he couldn't open the driver's door, he immediately called the dispatcher and requested the "jaws of life" be sent to separate the wreckage. This effort saved precious time, and quite possibly my life.

He saw that I had a full police escort to the local hospital and had all intersections on the way blocked so the ambulance could quickly pass through.

My injuries were many and severe. One of the paramedics later informed me that he had lost my pulse twice on the way to the hospital. I had thirteen broken ribs and a spleen rupture. Several broken ribs had pierced my lungs, necessitating a tracheotomy. There were also multiple face lacerations, a broken left jaw, and a significant eye injury, where a shattered bone around my left eye had perforated the eye, causing it to bleed. All these injuries, though, would eventually heal. An injury to the brainstem at the base of my right side of my head, however, would never improve.

At that time, every patrol car had a shotgun mounted vertically in the center of the vehicle. As my car was hit, my head struck the shotgun's barrel hard enough to put a visible dent in it. I was unconscious for three days due to the severity of that injury.

The left side of my body was impacted because the injury was to the right side of my brainstem. Being right-handed, I was relieved that my left side was damaged rather than my right.

Due to inadequate motor stability, I have had restricted use of my left arm and leg ever since. Even when I smiled, just the right side of my face responded.

When the attending physician told me I would have limited movement on the left side of my body, I mistakenly dismissed the diagnosis. I assumed I would recover completely with therapy. What I didn't comprehend however, was it wasn't my left arm and leg that were injured, but rather the part of my brain that sends movement signals.

After being released from the hospital, I tried to exercise and restore normal movement. After a few weeks, some of the scarring and discoloration faded, giving me false hope that I was making progress. I was so hopeful, in fact, that I felt ready to go back to work.

My department requested a medical release from my doctor before allowing me to return. I knew that if I stayed away from work too long, and these circumstances persisted, I would be encouraged to accept an early disability retirement. I reasoned that the only thing obvious was a slight limp with my left leg and I couldn't fully extend my left arm.

I went to the doctor who had treated me at the time of the accident to get permission to return to work. I knew I had to put on my best face and accept that I had not been completely honest with him. Following a brief physical checkup, he said I looked good, and it appeared I had made considerable improvement. He warned me I might have issues with equilibrium and memory lapses in the future. He told me that if I did, I should notify him.

After promising the doctor that I would start with limited duties, quite probably a desk job, he agreed to let me return to work. As I left his office, I glanced through the release form he gave me. There was no indication on the form that I should be assigned to limited or light duty, only that I may return to work. I was overjoyed.

When I returned to work, none of my supervisors or coworkers seemed to notice my limp or limited use of my left arm and leg. To my astonishment, I was put back on my former beat. I even started making disturbance calls again.

Practically everything was back to normal. Almost everything, except the way I was now handling my disturbance calls. Now more than ever, it was critical I ensure I never had to resort to physically restraining anyone. So, I took listening and internalizing the party's complaints to the next level. I constantly carried a clipboard containing complaint papers and was incredibly diligent about recording everyone's side. This method seemed to have calming effect as it showed people's accounts were being documented and would become official records.

For several weeks everything at work seemed to go well. However, things at home were not. My wife was furious at me for continuing to work in this field. My left arm had gotten so stiff that I needed her assistance getting dressed. Using my left hand, I couldn't button the sleeve on my right arm. But she did her best to help me without complaint. She only really protested when I asked her to help me with my gun belt. She had never been a fan of firearms.

It wasn't long before my supervisors started questioning me about what was wrong with my left leg. My justifications ranged from falling out of a tree while spraying for bagworms to taking a tumble down the stairs. The carriage of my left hand, folded behind my back, had become my trademark, and very few noticed anything unusual about it. My many excuses seemed to satisfy those who inquired. Almost everyone, except Sergeant Mill who had arrived on the scene and attempted to extract me from the wreckage.

According to department policy, when an officer stops a vehicle, the officer closest to his location must proceed to the area where the officer has the car stopped to assist him with his call. When I stopped a car for a traffic offense one day, I saw that the patrol car that arrived to back me up was that of Mills. After issuing a warning to the motorist and returning to my police car, Mills called me on the radio and asked me to meet him in the parking lot of a neighboring school.

Mills circled his patrol car in the school parking lot and pulled up to where our driver's doors were close together. We rolled down our windows. "Brown, are you okay?" Mike asked, looking me in the eyes. "Of course, Mike," I said, acting surprised. He went on to inquire whether there was anything wrong with my left arm. I replied that everything was fine. He then told me that he saw me getting in and out of my police car with my right hand reaching over and opening and closing the door. He also stated he had spotted me taking the person's driver's license with my right hand. I responded that I was not aware of it, and that it must have just been a rare occurrence. I don't think he bought my explanation. When I received a call from the dispatcher, I was thankful for the excuse to leave.

When I arrived at work the next day, there was a special department bulletin in my mailbox addressed to all officers. In the message, the Chief of Police, Chief Kilpatrick, declared his desire to form a new specialty unit. This unit would be in charge of dealing with family conflicts, as well as disturbances or fights in bars and nightclubs. It would, however, focus primarily on family disturbances and would be called the "Family Crisis Unit". Any officer who wished to be considered for the unit was urged to submit an officer's report expressing their wishes and listing any qualifications that would aid in their consideration. Because of my mobility issues, I did not submit an officer's report to be assigned to this new unit.

Throughout my four years with the department, I had garnered a reputation for successfully handling disturbance situations. My supervisors approached me practically every day and asked where my report was. I responded that I was working on it or that I had been so busy in court or school that I hadn't had time to submit it.

On one of my days off, a friend of mine, Sergeant Mannehill dropped by my home. Mannehill informed me that Chief Kilpatrick had asked him to meet me and find out why I had not submitted my officer's report to be assigned to the new Family Crisis Unit.

I could see my wife shaking her head as she stood behind MannehillI could see my wife shaking her head as she stood behind Mannehil. I asked him whether the Chief expected me to be on this new unit. He also told me that if I wanted to be on the new unit, the Chief had given him authority to tell me I would be accepted immediately.

Trying to avoid my wife's stern stare, I replied that Chief Kilpatrick was my employer, and if that was where he wanted me, then that was where I was going to be. To be honest, I was terrified that my wife would turn on me and divulge my medical problems at any moment. Fortunately, or unfortunately, depending on who was looking at it, she remained silent.

Before departing, Ron told me that myself and the other officers chosen for the unit would go to the County Mental Health Clinic the following week to begin a 30-day training program. The training would include classes with social workers, marriage counselors, and physiology professors, which would be overseen by Dr. Mance, Chairperson of the Psychology Department at Wichita State University.

I immediately began reasoning with my wife once Mannehill left. I think I convinced her that having other similarly trained officers with me would result in more peaceful outcomes. I also promised I would be especially cautious and that if my condition worsened, I would inform my supervisors.

During the training, I discovered the unit would have access to several connected agencies, including local ministers, marriage counselors, social workers, and mental health professionals. The training was excellent. The marriage counselors and social workers assisted us in learning reconciliatory techniques. The role-playing exercises were very beneficial in learning how to understand and react to differing opinions and viewpoints.

We were required to work 10-hour shifts. We were obliged to work those hours since it had been established most of the disturbances occurred between the hours of six o'clock at night and four o'clock in the morning. However due to the late and extended hours and the intensity of the work, we were only required to work four days a week. We were also given more time to complete these calls, which enabled us to spend more time on the scene trying to resolve the issue instead of making arrests and putting people in jail.

The new Family Crisis Unit also marked the introduction of our first two-man units. Initially, the officers would ride with new officers on a weekly basis. This was done to avoid personality clashes and continued until the officers were paired with companions who were compatible with them. Sixteen officers were selected for the unit. The city was divided into four quadrants, assigning each one a unit. The quadrants were rotated among the units until it was determined which units functioned best in specific areas.

I was partnered with Officer Howard, who had ridden with me as part of his training when he was a rookie recruit officer. We were assigned to an interracial neighborhood in town with a high rate of disturbances. We would work as many as five or six disturbances in a single shift. We formed a solid working relationship and learned to rely on one another. It only took a few weeks to see our unit was a success. My wife was even starting to unwind. At the very least, she would relax until I needed her help slipping my left arm into my shirtsleeve and strapping on my gun belt.

I dreaded the time of day when I had to dress and get ready for work. When my son, Jason, was home, I would try to enlist his help, usually in an area of the house where my wife was not present. We tended to have a better and sweeter departure if I could leave for work without her helping me dress.

One evening Officer Howard and I received a call from our dispatcher around 9:00 p.m. informing us of a disturbance involving a weapon. The address of the disturbance indicated that it was in the neighborhood where I'd grown up. As a matter of fact, it was only a few houses away from where my parents still lived.

We arrived at the scene and observed only one light on at the back of the house. We approached the front door and knocked. After no one answered, we looked through the small window on the door. A light turned on in the back of the house. Every few seconds, we heard what sounded like a thud, a noise similar to an axe hitting a tree.

As we looked closer, we noticed a woman and two small children huddled up against the wall. Another thud was heard. We then noticed a very tall and muscular American Indian man approach the wall where the woman and children were crouched beside. He then reached out and pulled what appeared to be a Bowie knife from the wall. The knife seemed to be half the length of my arm. If he was testing how close he could throw the knife at the woman and two children, he had terrible aim. I had a strong feeling he had no intention of harming them.

I took a deep breath and knocked on the door, introducing myself as a "Blood Brother." The large man, turning to face us, said I may come in and talk to him if I removed my gun belt and nightstick. Officer Howard and I exchanged glances. This was a violation of all departmental regulations. Then, I heard another thud. Officer Howard looked at me and informed me I didn't have a choice. I could easily remove my pistol belt with my right hand because all I had to do was reach down and unlatch it. I removed it and held it up so the man could see it.

He approached us from the front door, staggering slightly as he walked. He glared down at me, checking to see if what I held in my hand was indeed my gun belt. I noticed he had a very strong odor of alcohol on him. He told me to leave it on the porch. He then unlocked the front door and returned to the kitchen. I could hear the woman and the two children sobbing as I stepped inside.

Suddenly, I heard the woman scream and heavy footsteps approaching. At each stride, I could feel the floor move beneath me. I turned swiftly towards the direction of the scream, so rapidly that I lost my equilibrium, which was another physical issue I had been dealing with since the accident.

I felt myself falling. Instinctively, I grabbed the man's arm to keep me from falling, taking us both to the floor. I'm sure his inebriated state contributed to him falling with me and my being able to constrain him.

Officer Howard helped me move the man over onto his stomach. The woman had turned the lights on by this point. We attempted to get the handcuffs on him, however his wrists were at least twice as big as mine. It was like attempting to put the handcuffs around someone's ankle.

The man was sobbing at this point, and he begged us not to put him in restraints. I immediately explained we were there to listen and we didn't want to hurt him. I'm not sure if he was aware that we couldn't get the handcuffs around his wrists.

Officer Howard wasted no time in calling for backup. When he heard this, the man became very upset. He pleaded with us not lock him up. Not being able to successfully get the handcuffs fastened anyway, I assured him that if he remained calm, I would not put the restraints on, and he and I would ride in the patrol car together. This seemed to settle him down.

I asked Officer Howard to bring me my clipboard so I could make arrangements with the hospital. At first, he looked at me somewhat puzzled and then he realized what I was asking him to do.

Officer Howard radioed St. Francis Hospital and informed them that we suspected we had a person with a mental illness, and they should prepare a room in the hospital's psychiatric ward. He also requested that all available security officers be present when we arrived. Neither of us were looking forward to restraining this man and transporting him to the hospital.

While Officer Howard was arranging transport, I tried to put together some kind of report. After speaking with the woman, I discovered she was the man's wife, and the children were theirs. The man's name was Jim Goodriver, and he was on a 30-day leave from the Winfield Mental Institute, which is about 50 miles south of Wichita. I also discovered that he was a full-blooded Cherokee Indian and had been drinking at a local tavern that day.

American Indians, at least the ones I've met, aren't usually very tall. I may be one quarter American Indian at the most, and I'm just a hair under five eleven. Jim stood every bit of six foot five. He had unusually broad shoulders and a very powerful frame. He was what you would call ruggedly handsome, with coal-black shoulder length hair.

St. Francis Hospital was roughly a 15-minute drive. I sat beside Jim in the patrol car and started talking to him. He had calmed down considerably, but it was apparent he did not want to talk about his wife or children.

I warned Jim that I might get in trouble, but I had decided to transport him to St. Francis Hospital rather than the city jail. As we arrived at the hospital, I observed what appeared to be half a dozen hospital security officers. I hope this would not alarm Jim. I clapped him on the shoulder as I looked at him and remarked that we had quite a welcoming committee.

I assured Jim that if he kept his word and didn't cause us any problems, I would do the same and keep him from being put in jail. I told him I would make sure he got a nice room.

I walked Jim into the admissions room and down the corridor to the elevator which carried us to the ninth floor, which is the lock up floor. I kept talking to Jim the entire time.

When we exited the elevator, we were greeted by a male nurse. We followed him down the hall to Jim's room. Jim could see the containment straps on the bed. I had no idea how we were going to get him properly restrained.

His gown was on the bed. I handed it to him and told we would wait in the hall to give him some privacy while he changed. The nurse gave Officer Howard and me a disapproving look. I knew that if he refused to cooperate or became angry, we were in big trouble. But at this point, we were just going to have to trust Jim.

And, trusting him paid off. We returned to find Jim seated at the foot of the bed in his hospital gown. The nurse assisted him in lying back on the bed. I took one of the straps and wrapped it around his left wrist. Looking at me a little puzzled, Jim observed I was having trouble trying to get the strap fastened with my left hand. When Jim raised his right hand that was still free, I instinctively reached for my gun. I was hit with a jolt of shame as I realized he was simply trying to help me put the strap on.

The hard part came once we had secured him in bed. I tried, as tactfully as I could, to explain to Jim that Officer Howard and myself were going to have to leave and go back to work. I even told him that we had another call. I assured him that I would come back and see him. I told him I would make sure that some good people were going to look after him. Looking at the nurse, I asked him if he could get Jim some water and try to make him comfortable.

As Officer Howard and I exited the room and proceeded down the corridor, Jim called out, "Brown, I thought you were my friend." Friends don't leave friends tied up!" His words haunted me for many days to come.

I went to check on Jim the following weekend, which I had off. The hospital advised me that he had been transferred back to the Winfield Mental Institution and visitors were not being allowed. This bothered me more than I thought. I'd let myself become personally involved. The story surrounding this particular call had spread across the department. Officer Howard, who had witnessed the incident from the doorway, informed other officers that as Jim swung his knife at me, I grabbed his shirt and threw Jim to the floor. First and foremost, I don't believe I could have done so due to Jim's size and high level of intoxication. Second, due to my loss of equilibrium I was falling with Jim, not taking him down.

I couldn't refute Officer Howard's account, so I just let his version spread. Little did I know, however, that my months of moving carefully and making excuses were about to come to an end. It had been almost two years since my accident. Much to my disappointment, I hadn't been able to improve the movement on my left side. Despite exercising and prayer, if anything, my condition had worsened.

I don't know whether it was a result of making all these disturbance calls or not, but I was questioned almost daily about my limp. I was almost running out of excuses. One day, as I was walking by my Major's office, he called me in. He remarked that my ankle was taking a long time to heal. I had told him several months before that I had fallen out of a tree while trimming it.

The next day when I reported for duty and picked up my mail, there was an officer's report from Chief Kilpatrick. He asked to see me in his office. I found him in his office standing. He walked over to me and stopped about an arm's length away. Looking me right in the eye, he asked me to put both hands as high in the air as I could. I just stood there looking at him for a few seconds. He then asked me to pretend that he had a gun on me and was asking me to try and touch the sky. Repeating himself and getting a little louder, again he said, "Brown put both hands in the air. "

I felt a sense of dread in the pit of my stomach. I responded, raising my right hand all the way up, outstretched. My left hand, however, couldn't reach higher than my shoulder. He then asked, "If someone had a gun and was chasing you, could you run?" At this point, I thought the time for the excuses was over and I might as well tell the truth. I said, "Chief, if I was being chased up a flight of stairs I could run, not as fast as I used to, but if I were being chased down a flight of stairs, I would probably fall."

Kilpatrick reached out and put his arm around my shoulders and told me he was going to put me on departmental leave with pay until he could make arrangements for me to see some department physicians for a complete physical. Reaching out and shaking his hand, I replied that's fine, I needed a little time off anyway. I knew as I walked out of the Chief's office what the results of the examinations would be. I honestly felt a sense of peace and relief. I was tired of making excuses and being untruthful.

The Chief's assistant called me the following week. She informed me of the dates and times of my exams. I was referred to a neurologist and one of the local physicians chosen by the department. The neurology examination revealed all the physical problems I was experiencing. I was contacted by the

Chief's assistant a few days after the examinations and was told that the Chief wanted me to be available the following week. I knew in my heart this couldn't be good.

A week passed and I met with the Chief. I could tell he was not his usual happy self. He informed me that both doctors' evaluations indicated that my left side was moderately to severely incapacitated. He also informed me that my neurological evaluation revealed that I was prone to blackouts and balance issues.

Looking me in the eyes, the Chief said he hoped to be able to offer me a desk job, but that the findings concerning blackouts would not allow it. A police officer is required to carry a firearm and to wear one inconspicuously when not on duty. He said if there was any possibility of me blacking out, I could not have a weapon.

He informed me that I had received one of the highest scores on the most recent lieutenant's test. He stated that he had searched all his administrative positions for an opportunity for me and nothing was available at the time. He said he had gone over my case with Major Blevins and was confident I would be awarded early disability retirement. He said he now understood why I had never turned in my officer's report for the Family Crisis Unit. Before leaving his office, he let me know how sorry he was, and how much he appreciated my efforts in making the Family Crisis Unit a success.

At the next City Commission meeting Major Blevins argued for my early retirement. A motion was made, and I was granted early disability retirement. My short tenure with the Wichita Police Department had come to an end.

Chapter 2

"The Journey"

While an important chapter of my life had come to end, little did I know that my real life's journey was about to begin.

My wife got her real estate license and worked for one of the city's top real estate companies. She excelled in her new field and was among Wichita's most successful realtors. Her earnings would soon surpass mine.

Her success changed our roles. She was the breadwinner, and I was a househusband. And, while I took advantage of my newfound spare time by earning a double degree in Administration of Justice majoring in both administration and investigation, I can't say that I cherished my new role. But it did keep things moving in a positive and peaceful way for the next 10 years. Jason majored in psychology from Wichita State University. Renee moved to Southern California after graduating from the University of Kansas with a degree in journalism. My wife and I continued to visit my brother and his wife in Colorado each year. In fact, it was my positive experiences and the unbridled beauty of southwestern Colorado that fueled the next steps that would eventually make Colorado home and epicenter of what I call a spiritual transformation.

My brother, Fred, taught high school biology in Cortez. Strong agricultural traditions and American Indian heritage characterize this southwestern town located eight miles from the entrance to Mesa Verde National Park, not far from the Four Corners area. Fred did guided tours in Mesa Verde National Park in the summer when he wasn't teaching.

Every time we visited; I would accompany my brother to the Anasazi Indian Ruins. These ancient cliff dwellings fascinated me and made me feel connected to this beautiful and mystical land.

Before heading back to Wichita, I asked Fred to notify me of any security or law enforcement openings in neighboring small towns. He knew how much I loved the area and looking at me with a big smile, he said he would definitely let me know.

Just a few weeks later, my brother sent me a help wanted ad from the local Cortez newspaper. Towaoc needed a security chief. My brother said Towaoc was home to the Ute Mountain Ute Tribe Reservation 12 miles south of Cortez.

Towaoc lies in the majestic shadow of the Sleeping Ute Mountains. From afar, this range looks like an American Indian sleeping on his back with one arm over his chest. From the northern part of Cortez, one may see a head feather behind his head and his feet pointing higher on the mountain range. Traveling west on Highway 160 between Mancos and Cortez, or west of the Mesa Verde National Park entrance, offers the best views.

I called my brother immediately about the job. I wanted to learn more before talking to my wife. My brother thought it was a Bureau of Indian Affairs job. My brother had met some of the Council members while refereeing basketball games at their recreation center and was confident that they would be the ones interviewing the applications.

I needed to discuss the possibility of relocating with my wife. Being open and honest was one of the reasons our 27-year marriage had endured. I hoped she would let me explore this new opportunity.

So, after getting my thoughts together, I introduced the idea of moving and a new career for me. She said she would be giving up a career that took her years to build and that Cortez was a much smaller community than she was used to. However, after taking a long pause she told me to follow my heart and apply. She said she looked forward to not working and exploring new hobbies. I felt confident that this path was the right path.

My wife reviewed my application and asked why I left the medical portion blank. She warned me that if they contacted the Wichita Police Department, they would reveal my physical limitations.

Since the Head of Security was a management role and the position description didn't include carrying a firearm, I did not include my medical history. I also told her I would be happy to turn over my health records, if asked.

The following day, I mailed the resume to the address, which appeared in the ad, and with my brother's advice put it to the attention of Mr. Truman House. My brother had advised me that he was head chairman of the tribal Council.

After three weeks passed, I assumed they offered to position to someone else. Maybe it wasn't for me. If it didn't work out, maybe something better was in store for me. Then, the phone rang. My wife answered and told me Truman House was calling from Towaoc. Both surprised and delighted, I took the phone. Mr. House informed me that the other six Council members had viewed my application and wanted to meet me. I agreed to an interview for the following Tuesday at 10:00 a.m. The wheels were in motion.

It was the last week in September and I knew my wife would enjoy visiting Colorado when the aspens were at their peak colors. Cortez was a two-day drive from Wichita, so we decided to leave the following Friday so we would have time to visit with my brother and his wife.

The two-day drive was relaxing and the turning colors were spectacular. As we approached Cortez on Highway 160, the sun was just setting over the Sleeping Ute. I didn't remember the silhouette being quite so large. But there lay the sleeping giant, with his arm resting over his heart. I was suddenly struck with the feeling of coming home.

Years ago, the early Utes of this area had a legend about this mysterious cluster of mountains, which make up the silhouette of the Sleeping Ute. According to legend, a great Ute Warrior came to fight the evil ones of that time who were causing trouble. A tremendous battle ensued between the Great Warrior and the evil ones. The Great Warrior was hurt in the battle and lay down to rest. While resting, he fell into a deep sleep and the blood from his wounds turned into living waters for all the creatures to drink.

The American Indians believe the Great Warrior is pleased with his people when clouds gather on the highest peak, which is formed by his arm across his chest. He lets rain and wind slip through his pockets. Even today, Ute Indians in this area use the Sleeping Ute Mountain and the location of where the clouds are in relation to his pockets to forecast the coming weather.

Ute Tribes believe someday the Great Warrior will awaken. They believe he will rise up in a time of great need and help his people. They believe the Great Warrior will protect them, giving them inspiration and guidance. The Ute Mountains are very sacred to them, and they often refer to the Sleeping Ute Mountain as the Great Warrior.

As my wife and I continued our drive toward Cortez, the Sleeping Ute almost appeared as if he were moving ever so slightly. This was due to our vantage point and the changing colors as the sun was setting, but it heightened the mystical quality of the moment.

Sunday night we arrived at my brother's house as planned. Betty, his wife, served us a delicious dinner. As we ate and caught up, we all remarked what a remarkable change this would be, to relocate in a town where my brother had lived for over 25 years. After not seeing him much, it would be great to live where we could do things together again.

Monday, we picnicked and fished. Fishing was my brother's way of relaxing. On past visits we got in a habit of taking his boat to a nearby lake nestled in the mountains called Lake McFee. My wife and he would usually catch around 20 fish each. I might catch four or five. My wife and my brother had contests for who caught the first, the most and the largest. This year, once again my wife and brother reeled in the most fish.

The Sleeping Ute was visible as we drove home. My brother said that the Ute Mountain Ute Tribe Council building where I would be interviewing the next morning, was located at the base of the mountain range that resembles the Sleeping Ute's arm resting over his chest.

He told me there was only one road in, and that I couldn't get lost. He said he didn't remember the name of the street, but that the tribal office building was on the main road and the front of the building was marked with the address of 525. He also said I would pass by the new security office, which was a white stucco building on my way to the Council building.

We all went out to dinner that evening to a restaurant within the Mesa Verde National Park. My brother was still working for the Park Service, and enjoyed going to the restaurant, which set at the top of the Mesa. From the restaurant you had a panoramic view of the surrounding area. He had a table reserved for us by a window facing south. He pointed out a unique rock formation in the distance resembling a boat, aptly named Shiprock. I was once again struck by the beauty of this place, and how I very much wanted this job to work out.

As I went to sleep that night, I was trying to imagine what the Council building would look like, and what questions might be asked. I gained some peace when I decided to stop trying to imagine all the possible outcomes and circumstances and trust that God would guide me. If this was the right move, then God wouldn't abandon me. With that thought, I fell into a peaceful sleep.

Chapter 3

"A New Adventure"

After breakfast, I started for Towaoc a little early. I didn't want to be late. As I entered the small downtown area, one of the first buildings I saw was the security building. It was a large, one-story, white stucco building with the American flag displayed on the front grounds.

I drove on to what appeared to be the center of the town. There I saw a three-story beige brick building on one side of the small, town square. This building seemed to be the newest building in town. A sign reading Ute Mountain Ute Tribe Council Chambers let me know I'd found my destination.

I glanced at my watch and noticed I was about a half hour early. I decided to pass the time by exploring the small downtown area. I had dressed somewhat casually for my interview, wearing dark slacks and a light-colored sport coat. I figured a short walk wouldn't mess me up too bad.

Walking around the square, I noticed a small diner with "Merna's" painted on the front window. It looked like a nice place to grab to bite. I also passed by what looked like a large activity center with several young people hanging around. I assumed this was where my brother refereed basketball games.

When I approached a light green building with "Suma's Hardware" written on the large window in the front, a strong gust of wind blew down the center of the street, moving through my hair and billowing out my sport coat. There was an old American Indian man with long white hair braided down his back, sitting in a chair in front of Suma's Hardware. He had a bright yellow blanket draped around his shoulders. I waved at him and got a peaceful smile in return.

Back at the Council building, I located the interview room on the directory. Along the way I noticed a nice-looking middle-aged man with a thick braid of gray-black hair that hung just below his shoulders. He appeared to be about my age and size and was wearing a turquoise-colored shirt and blue jeans. He extended his hand to shake mine and said, "You must be Mr. Brown." "I am Truman House, head of the Council. I'm glad you made it safe and sound." He then invited me into the Council chambers.

Upon entering I saw six other men at a long table. They all seemed be about my age, except for one man who seemed about 10 years older. Truman invited me to sit down in a chair next to where he was standing. As I sat down, he introduced me to the group.

They all were looking over copies of my application. The man who appeared to be the oldest of the group broke the silence and asked about my American Indian background, which I had mentioned in my application. I replied that I didn't know exactly how much American Indian blood I had but that my mother's parents were half American Indian, each from a different tribe. I continued telling them my grandmother on my mother's side was born on an Indian Reservation in Sioux City, Iowa, and was Lakota Sioux. Her father's mother was from Oklahoma and was half Cherokee. I explained how I had met her when I was a small boy. Her name was Talulla Crow. I told the Council that she was beautiful and kind and that one of my mother's brothers had grown up on a reservation near Norman, Oklahoma. I told them that my father wasn't American Indian; he was Scotch-Irish. Looking at me with a smile, the man who asked the question didn't reply but nodded as if he understood.

After what seemed to be a long, drawn-out silence, one of the younger Council members broke the silence and asked me why I had chosen to apply for a position almost 1000 miles away from my home, and why I had chosen to work on a reservation. I replied by telling him that I had a brother who lived in Cortez, who had told me about the position. After I mentioned his name and told them that he refereed a lot of their basketball games at their recreation center, some of the members said they knew him. I also said that I had visited this area of Colorado many times and loved this part of the country. I continued saying with our children grown and living their own lives, my wife and I decided we'd like a change of pace and scenery.

The same man then asked me to elaborate on my training and experiences in law enforcement. After hitting my career highlights, I mentioned that I had extensive experience interacting with people of all races and felt I would get along with the people here on the reservation.

One of the other Council members responded, "You know we have occasional fights and disturbances in our community. Would that bother you?" I responded by saying, "Interesting you should ask." I told them about my last assignment with the Wichita Police Department that involved nothing but working disturbances. I explained I had been selected for a special team called the Family Crisis Unit based on my record of successfully working disturbance calls.

I told him I never had a set way of working these disturbance calls because each was different and involved completely different circumstances. The approach that worked in one situation sometimes wouldn't work in another. I told him that one must keep in mind that these disturbances are sometimes profoundly upsetting to those involved. I found that if I was patient and truly listened to what both parties had to say, even if it was quite evident who was most at fault, and if I treated both parties like I would expect to be treated, things usually worked out.

I could tell by the looks on their faces that they were pleased by my response. Truman then said that besides being head of security, I would represent their people and be their spokesman with the federal and local authorities. Truman said, "By this, I mean you would head up the Bureau of Indian Affairs on the reservation."

One of the other Council members spoke up saying, "Mr. Brown, the Ute Mountain Ute Tribe Reservation is a sovereign nation. We are a nation within a nation." He continued, "This reservation came into existence in 1903 by a treaty signed with the American government, and no other law enforcement agency has any power on this reservation and can only come on our property if we ask for their assistance." I learned this Council member's name was Jim Yancey. Mr. Yancey was quite outspoken regarding the rights of the reservation and their nation. He spoke with much pride regarding the sovereign status they enjoyed.

I would later learn just how right Mr. Yancey was about this reservation being a sovereign nation. I would find that the reservation's sovereignty, clearly stated in the 1903 treaty with our government and the Ute Indian leaders, was perhaps my reason for being here. It might even be my reason for existing, at least at this point in my journey.

Another Council member spoke up and said that it would be helpful for them, and me too, if I could attend a Council meeting once a month. I agreed with the man, whose name

I learned was Mr. Hannon, and said I would be happy to. Truman then spoke up and said that I would also be expected to check with the head of the Council following each of their monthly meetings.

Truman continued telling me that if the Council had any federal or local requests, I would be informed, either at their meetings or immediately following. Truman further advised if I were selected for this position, I would be deputized by the Montezuma County Sheriff. He said I would have three deputies under me.

After about 10 minutes of cordial conversation, Truman asked if I would mind waiting outside in the hall while the Council discussed the interview and made their decision. I was somewhat surprised by how quickly this was moving. I had expected to see more people applying for the position. I respected the forthrightness and frankness of Truman and the Council members.

While I waited, I found a chair and sat down to relax. A sense of peace came over me as I realized that if this was the right move then it would work out. Of course, this would not only have to be a blessing for me, but also what was best for the Council and the Towaoc community. Both parties need to be blessed.

As I thought back over the decisions I had made in my life, the ones that had worked out the best were the ones where I was able to lay aside my human reasoning and rely on God for answers. I must have sat there for some 20 minutes meditating about the good that could come from getting this position, when the door opened. A smiling Truman emerged with his hand extended to shake mine. As he shook my hand he said, "Congratulations, Security Chief Brown." He continued, telling me that all the Council members were impressed with my background and how I handled the interview, agreeing I was the right man for the job. I responded saying, "Mr. House, it will be an honor to serve the residents of the Ute Mountain Ute Tribe reservation." Truman said, "Please Robert, just call me Truman."

Truman then walked down the hall toward a vending machine and asked me if I'd like to have soda with him to celebrate. I said, "absolutely I would." As I riffled through my pockets for change, Truman just smiled at me and said, "Don't worry Brown, it's on the House!" We both laughed and cracked open our sodas and toasted. I have to say that was the best soda I'd ever had.

While we enjoyed our sodas, Truman asked if I would be able to start in one week. He said he realized this didn't give me much time to find a house and settle, but the position had been vacant for so long, they really needed to have me in place. I told him a week is fine and because my wife and I were staying with my brother we could take our time looking for our new home.

After going over my duties and discussing some of the challenges that went with the job, Truman said if I had the time, he would like to show me the security headquarters and introduce me to two of my deputies. I replied, "Absolutely!"

Still somewhat in shock over the quick decision, I accompanied Truman to the door. As we walked outside, again a strong gust of wind suddenly came up from out of nowhere. It blew Truman's big black western hat off and out in the middle of the street. As we continued on our way to the security building, we walked by Suma's Hardware. The old American Indian man with the long white hair was still sitting there. Truman noticed me looking at him and said, "That's Jake. He's one of our tribal elders. Some people consider him to be a holy man." Walking towards Jake, Truman called back at me, "Come on, I'll introduce you."

When we reached the man called Jake, Truman said, "Hello, Jake." Looking at Truman and me, the man nodded a greeting and smiled. I noticed his eyes were bright blue, which I found unusual. Truman then introduced me as the new Security Chief. I extended my hand and shook Jake's. Looking at me with a smile in his eyes, Jake asked, "What did you think of that gust of wind?" Smiling, I replied, "I thought it was going to blow Truman and me away!" I asked Jake if they had sudden wind gusts like that often. Jake replied, "Just when the Great Spirit wants our attention." Jake then asked me what I thought of their community. I replied that I liked what I had seen so far. I told Jake I enjoyed meeting him and looked forward to seeing him again soon.

Catching up with Truman, we passed "Merna's", the little diner that caught my eye as I was exploring the town earlier. Turning to me, Truman commented, "Merna's has some real tasty food." With the security building being just a stone's throw away, I had a feeling I'd be one of Merna's best customers.

Upon entering the security building I was greeted by a light-skinned American Indian man, about 3 inches shorter than me, with a crew cut. He was wearing a white uniform shirt and faded blue jeans. I noticed numerous badges hanging from the top of his left pocket. The only two I recognized were a Red Cross badge and a marksmanship badge. On his left sleeve were four light blue hash stripes representing the years he had served with the department.

Truman introduced me to the man as his new boss. Then he introduced the deputy to me as Deputy Pinky Irontail. Looking at me with a smile, Pinky said he was glad to meet me and shook my hand. I told him I was looking forward to working with him and realized I had much to learn about their community and would need him to help learn the ropes. This seemed to sit well

Pinky, and he flashed me a big grin, nodding and saying, "Sure boss, I'd be more than happy to."

An American Indian man I assumed to be another one of my deputies walked towards me an extended his hand saying, "I'm Deputy Paul Wolf. It's a pleasure to meet you Mr. Brown." "Please call me Robert, or you can just call me Brown," I responded as I shook his hand. Paul was lean and muscular and taller than me. I estimated him to be about 6'3". I laughed to myself thinking if you stood Pinky, myself, and Paul side by side, we'd look like a staircase. Paul was wearing the same white uniform shirt as Pinky although he didn't have as many badges on his pocket. I noticed five light blue hash stripes on his sleeve, one more than Pinky.

Both deputies had their gun belts off and draped across the back of their desk chairs. The firearms in their belts appeared to be .38 calibers. Pinky's had white pearl handle. Each belt also had short batons and a handcuff pouch.

As I glanced around the office, I couldn't help but notice how cluttered it was. Two file drawers were pulled open in one of the four cabinets against one of the walls. The wastebasket by the desk where Pinky sat was running over. The floors that were a hodgepodge of carpet and tile, looked like they hadn't seen a vacuum or mop in years. I figured I'd tackle the cleaning later.

Paul informed me it was his day to serve as the dispatcher. I asked him if he had received many calls. He replied that he had only six all morning. I could hear radio traffic on his radio. As I listened to it, I assumed that it was either the neighboring town of Cortez, the County Sheriff, or perhaps both. Hanging over Paul's desk was a large map of the town of Towaoc.

Turning toward me, Truman said he would leave me with my two deputies, as he had to get back to the Council meeting because they were making some decisions about the activity center today. I thanked Truman for showing me around and making me feel at home and told him I was in good hands with Pinky and Paul.

After Truman left, Paul informed me his brother Jay came in at 4:00 p.m. I told Paul I would hang around to meet him. If Jay came on at 4:00 p.m., he probably got off at midnight. I was curious about who worked the late shift. In Wichita, this was the time when a lot of crime happened. I asked Pinky and Paul what they did about covering the time from midnight until the morning when the day shift began. I assumed they came on at 7:00 a.m. Pinky spoke up and said that the County Sheriff's dispatcher had their telephone numbers and called them if anything serious happened. I wanted to ask what they did to ensure coverage on their days off. But I didn't want to be that guy who shows up and wants to change everything, so I decided to wait until we all got to know each other better.

I knew, however, that I was going to have to come up with a feasible plan which would allow someone to be on duty 24 hours a day, seven days a week. And the plan would need to accomplish this goal without causing a radical change. I would come up with a schedule to cover all three work shifts, and have each deputy rotate his workdays to cover the others' days off. If I expressed enough confidence in them to handle the evening and night shifts by themselves, I could get them to agree to my new ideas. I would have to be the one in charge of the daytime shift due to my other responsibilities and availability to the Council.

I decided to leverage a three-pronged approach I used in my police work in Wichita. First, I introduce the idea as a solution. Second, I convince them why it's a good solution. And, last but certainly not least, I include them in the decision-making. I had found this approach to work so well settling disturbances that sometimes the guilty party would practically put themselves in handcuffs.

In the meantime, I would leave a notice with the County Sheriff's dispatcher to always contact me first on serious calls, especially at night.

My thoughts were interrupted by Pinky, who announced it was his turn to go to early lunch. Pinky asked if I would like to join him, telling me that the special at Merna's that day was pot roast. I told Pinky pot roast would hit the spot.

I asked Paul if he wanted us to bring him something from Merna's. He replied that he planned to go to Merna's when we returned.

As we entered Merna's several patrons stopped talking and eating and turned to look at Pinky and me. It was mildly uncomfortable, but understandable. Afterall, I don't imagine they see many new folks. Towaoc isn't exactly a tourist destination. After waiting perhaps five minutes, a pretty Native American woman approached us and asked to seat us. She was about 5'7", slender, and wore her raven black hair in a tight bun at the back of her neck.

Once seated, she handed us a menu and told us that the day's special was pot roast. Looking at her with his smile, Pinky commented, "Merna, that's why we're here. But first, I want to introduce you to my new boss, Mr. Robert Brown." Turning toward me, Merna had a look of surprise on her face. I told her I had heard about how good the food was here and was looking forward to experiencing it myself. As she walked away, her look of surprise changed to a smile.

Almost immediately, a petite young lady with her long black hair secured in braids, set two glasses of water down. She asked, "What will it be?" Pinky told the waitress, "We want two specials, Vonna." He then added, "and bring two coffees." I asked Vonna to please bring cream and sugar, telling her I have a terrible sweet tooth. This made her smile. Pinky spoke up as Vonna wrote down our order, saying, "This is Mr. Brown, our new Security Chief." Turning in my direction and giving me a quick once over, Vonna commented, "You don't look like a cop, Mr. Brown." I smiled and told Vonna that I was going to give it a try. She walked away and said she would be back shortly with our order. I noticed Pinky grinning from ear to ear as he watched her walk away.

It wasn't long before Vonna returned with two huge plates brimming with pot roast, mashed potatoes, and gravy. She said to save some room for Merna's boysenberry pie. I told her to hold a couple of pieces for us and thanked her for remembering I had a sweet tooth.

We were done in just 30 minutes. I left Vonna a nice tip, and Pinky let me pay the check. As we walked back to the office, I noticed the chair where Jake had been sitting was vacant. I was looking forward to visiting with him. When we arrived at our office, I told Pinky to go on, that I wanted to walk through the downtown area and meet some of the business owners.

I passed by Suma's Hardware and could see John working in the rear of the store. I walked by a couple of buildings that were boarded up. One looked like it might have been a bicycle shop.

Down at the end of the main road was a one-story building with faded blue paint. Across the front window was the name Autry's. As I walked in, I was greeted by the sound of pool balls hitting each other and raucous laughter. Looking over in the direction the noise came from, I observed two young American Indian men playing pool. There were about six pool tables in the room and about a dozen chairs. One of the chairs was occupied by a huge American Indian man. I couldn't see his face very well as his head was hanging down as if he were asleep. He was quite large, however. Sitting down, I judged him to be at least six-and-a-half feet tall.

A fellow about my size, wearing an apron, walked toward me. As he approached, he extended his hand to shake mine and said, "I'm William Autry; just call me Bill." I shook his hand and said, "I'm Robert Brown. I've just accepted the Security Chief position." He motioned over at the large man slumped in the chair saying, "I'm glad you dropped by."

Bill told me his establishment was where people came to play pool, ping-pong, and cards and socialize and visit. I realized he was walking me toward the front door as we were speaking. Upon reaching the front door, he stepped outside and motioned me to join him. He then informed me he recently had trouble with the large man I had noticed but couldn't get a look at as he had his head down.

Bill told me that he didn't serve alcohol, but the large man was drunk most of the time, saying he thought he was getting alcohol in Cortez or from friends.

I told Bill that while I was there, I'd have a word with him. Bill said if I was going to talk to that man, I should have my deputies join me. I assured him it would be fine, I just wanted to visit with him.

As I walked away toward the fellow, Bill said, half under his breath, "Don't make him mad." About 10 feet before I reached the man, my left foot almost went out on me, and I kicked the leg on one of the chairs. I usually maintained good control of my left side paralysis, but occasionally my left leg buckles and almost goes out from under me.

The noise I made caused the large man to raise his head and look at me. As he looked at me, I couldn't believe my eyes. It had been over nine years since I removed this man from his home and left him in a psychiatric ward in Wichita. His hair had turned steel gray and hung down to just above his shoulders. This man was none other than Jim Goodriver.

Chapter 4

"Old Acquaintances"

I couldn't believe it. What in the world was Jim doing on the Ute Mountain Ute Tribe Reservation? I continued to study him as I cautiously stepped closer. Maybe it was the lighting, I told myself, as it was dark in the back of the room. I must admit, I was hoping that once I got closer, I would discover this man was someone else and not Jim.

Then the large man opened his eyes, stood up slowly and said, "Is that you, Brown?" Brown, what are you doing here?" Jim then stepped toward me and picking me up off my feet, gave me a big hug. By this time, a total silence had come over the room and I could see Bill out of the corner of my eye, watching us in utter astonishment. As Jim put me down, I reached out to shake his hand. His large hand swallowed mine.

As we stood there shaking each other's hands, I knew Bill was concerned, so I called over to him and told him that I knew Jim from Wichita, Kansas. Turning my attention to Jim, I told him how good it was to see him. Jim, still looking surprised, asked me what I was doing there. I told him that I was forced into early retirement with the Wichita Police Department, had relatives in Cortez, and I had accepted a new job here on the reservation. Looking at Jim, I told him that I was going to be the new Chief of Security.

Much to my surprise, Jim responded by saying, "Good, I always liked you, Brown." I asked Jim what he was doing so far from Wichita. I also told him that I thought he was Cherokee. Jim replied that the hospital I took him to in Wichita had sent him back to the psychiatric institution in Winfield. Jim said he gained a release from Winfield by coming out here in his brother's custody. He said that his brother had married a Ute Indian woman who lived on the reservation and that they had two children.

Maybe it was because I hadn't seen him in so long, but it looked as though Jim had grown a few inches and put on about 50 pounds. I asked him if he would walk outside with me because I wanted to visit with him a little longer. After walking a few steps outside, I turned to Jim and asked him what he was doing now to keep busy. Outside of snow removal and filling in potholes, he said he had not found any steady work. Looking at me somewhat seriously and raising his voice slightly, Jim said, "You know Brown, every time I start a new job, everyone treats me like I am just some big dumb Indian."

I glanced over to my new office building and saw Pinky and Paul watching us through the front window. Then an idea came to me. Remembering how messy our headquarters was I remarked to Jim, "You know Jim, I have something in mind." What do you think of custodial work and possibly running some local errands for our office?" I told him I couldn't promise anything and that I'd need to check with the Council first, but as far as I was concerned the job was his if he wanted it.

Jim didn't say anything, he simply stared at me. I told him I'd bring it before the Council at their next meeting. I then asked Jim if he would give me an address and phone number where he could be reached in case the Council liked my idea.

But I also wanted to know where I could get in touch with him anyway, now that he was back in my life again. After what seemed like a long pause, Jim gave me his brother's address and phone number.

As I turned to leave, I reached out and patted Jim on the shoulder and said, "Jim, this was really a pleasant surprise running into you here." I also told him that I had thought about him a lot over the past nine years. I said, "Jim, if you ever need me, or anything is troubling you, come and get me." He was silent, but I thought I caught a slight glimmer in his eyes as he reached out to shake my hand.

After returning to the office, I greeted Pinky and Paul. Looking at my watch I saw I had another hour before Jay came in. I felt this would be a good time to go through some of the files. Things were quiet for about an hour, then Pinky broke the silence by asking if I knew the large man I'd been talking to outside Autry's. Pinky and Paul were both staring at me intently, anticipating my response. I told them the man's name was Jim Goodriver and I had met him in Wichita, Kansas. He was involved in a disturbance call I was on. Paul interjected, "Yeah, I'm sure." I continued and told them about the incident. I said, "You can't imagine how surprised I was to see him here."

"Now we know who to call the next time we have trouble with him," Paul said. I asked Paul what he meant by that. Pinky elaborating by saying he, Paul, and Jay were all called the last time Jim was intoxicated and behaving erratically. He went on to say that they couldn't control him, and the Montezuma County Sheriff's Office had to send four police officers to help. They also had social workers and doctors from the hospital. No one seemed to have control of the situation until Jim's brother came and talked to him. The Council, according to Paul, discussed the matter at their next meeting and concluded that if it happened again, they would ask him and his brother to leave the reservation. When they were finished, I informed them that if anything like that ever happened again, I wanted to be called. I wrote down my phone number and posted it on the bulletin board behind Pinky's desk.

I then turned my attention to the doors, as a somewhat heavyset man in a white uniform shirt entered with a bit of a noisy flourish. My third and final deputy Jay Wolf, Paul's brother had arrived. I noticed his shirt didn't carry many patches, but he had eight bars, marking Jay as my most senior deputy.

I approached Jay and extended my hand. "Jay, this is Mr. Brown, our new boss," Paul said before I could identify who I was. Jay smiled and reached out to shake my hand. Jay wasn't quite as tall as Paul, but he was taller than six feet.

After visiting with Jay for a few minutes, I got up and waved in their direction and told them I was going home to unpack. I let them know I was very impressed with all three of them and was looking forward to working together. As I walked down the street, I glanced over to Suma's Hardware. Jake's chair was vacant. I couldn't help but wonder if he saw my encounter with Jim.

As I drove back to my brother's place, I couldn't help but note how beautiful the sun made the Sleeping Ute Mountain range and the town of Towaoc appear in my rearview mirror.

When I arrived at my brother's house, I was greeted by Belinda, Fred, and Betty. They were surprised to hear that I had been hired for the position so quickly and had already spent one day on the job. I explained that I didn't need to return until next Monday. My wife then told me that the movers had called and left a message, saying they could be there as early as next Saturday. She also told me that she had found three houses she wanted me to see. The one she seemed to like best was vacant and only about six blocks from my brother's house. It was a new home and had a beautiful view of the Sleeping Ute from the back deck. I couldn't believe how things were falling so perfectly into place. I looked at their three smiling faces and announced I was taking them all to dinner. My offer was enthusiastically accepted by all.

Over the next few days, Belinda showed me the homes she had picked out. I agreed with her, the newer home with the view of the Sleeping Ute was the best choice. The fact that we could put down a deposit and move in when our furniture arrived on Saturday made it even more appealing.

The house was located a little further west than my brother's home and would save a few minutes on my commute time. The deck ran the entire length of the back of the home with an excellent view of the Sleeping Ute and I could just make out where the Main Street of Towaoc was below the Sleeping Ute's chest. Belinda advised me that this home was in the best area of town and had a popular floor plan. After being in real estate for over 17 years, she was already thinking "resale." She said we could close on the home on Friday. She said she had also located a good fitness center in Cortez and was already starting to make friends. I was happy to see how well she was adjusting to a smaller town and slower pace.

Everything moved along smoothly the next six days, but also very quickly. Here it was Sunday evening already, and I would be going to work in the morning. Belinda interrupted my thoughts and asked me to come see the beautiful sunset from our deck. The sun had set behind the Sleeping Ute's arm folded over his chest. Over almost the entire length of his body was a silver lining, with shades of yellow, orange and lavender.

After a restful night's sleep, I awoke eager to get to work. As I drove though the downtown area, I found myself looking for Jake. I noticed his chair was empty. It was about 9:00 a.m. when I walked into the office. Jay was the only one there. I asked him where he and the others had gotten their uniform shirts. He replied that it was at a uniform shop in Cortez, called "Brick's." I then asked Jay what time most of the businesses opened in Towaoc. He replied 9 a.m., although Autry's usually didn't open until 10 a.m. I asked Jay to remind me to get everyone together to set up a work schedule and days off. I told them the schedule I was thinking about would be a little different. Jay asked what I meant.

I proceeded to lay out my plan, using my famous three-prong approach. I explained it was necessary for me to be there during the day, for the Council's sake. I explained further that if they could decide which one wanted the evening shift and which one wanted the late shift, that perhaps the other one could work on a rotation basis on their days off. Jay replied that it sounded good to him and that he would be happy to work the late shift. He said he didn't think Pinky or Paul liked it.

I thanked Jay and told him he had taken a big load off my mind, as I didn't know which one to ask to work the late shift. I told him that he could go ahead and take off now that I was there. Pinky and Paul walked in and before I had a chance to greet them, Jay announced, "Brown said he was going to assign me the late shift, and one of you will work the 2nd shift." He then tried to explain how the rotation would work.

I interrupted at that point and told Pinky and Paul the reasons I felt I should take the day shift. They all agreed, and, without further questions, Pinky spoke up and told us this was to be his day off anyway, and that if Paul wanted the evening shift, he would take the rotation shifts. Paul said that would be fine with him. I told all three of them that I had been worrying about this all week and never dreamed it would work out so well. I also told them since they had all been so flexible, I was going to see about getting a coffee pot and perhaps someone to clean the office occasionally. I didn't dare tell them who I had in mind.

We all walked out of the office together. I said I would try to gather all the business contact information that day, and that it would give me a good opportunity to meet all the business owners.

Glancing up the street, I saw that Jake was in his chair again. He was positioned so he could bask in the sun and had a crimson red blanket draped over his shoulders. Today he did not bother to braid the long white hair that fell past his shoulders.

I found Jake's presence very calming. He exuded contentment and always had a small smile playing across his face. I could see why he was held in such high esteem by the township. I felt now was as good a time as any to properly introduce myself and spend some time with this mysterious and gentle soul.

Chapter 5

"Footsteps of Truth"

Little did I know at the time, but I was about to embark on a life-changing journey with the most fascinating and wise man I would ever know. Upon reaching the spot where he was sitting, I greeted him, calling him "Sir." As he turned and looked at me with deep and searching eyes, in a kind, soft voice he asked, "How are you today, Mr. Brown?" I replied that I was feeling great.

Continuing to search me with his eyes, Jake then asked me the question that nobody on the Council or any of my deputies, or any one I had met in Towaoc had asked. "I see that you have a slight limp with your left leg and favor your left arm. What happened, Mr. Brown?" It had been nearly ten years since my accident, I had a lot of time to learn how to walk and appear normal. Unless you knew what happened, most likely you wouldn't suspect anything was wrong. However, Jake saw right through me.

Somehow, in the presence of this man, I knew it would be impossible to be untruthful or make excuses. I also didn't feel threatened by his question. So, I said I was in a car accident while serving on the Wichita Police Department and the accident had left me with a partially paralyzed left side.

Jake then asked what it was about the accident that left me partially paralyzed. I explained to him that patrol cars in Wichita carried the shotguns in an upright position in the center of the front seat. Somehow the barrel of the shotgun had bent over the backside of my head during the near fatal crash. Jake meekly interrupted me and said, "It must have damaged the right side of your brain stem." He was exactly right. I was surprised he knew this. Looking at him, somewhat in shock, I replied, "Exactly, sir."

As we continued talking, I couldn't help but observe what mastery of the English language he had. His grammar and diction were perfect. I also learned Jake held two master's degrees: one in religion and one in history. He said he attended college as a young man at neighboring community and state colleges in Durango, Colorado, located about 60 miles away.

I was awestruck by this man. I could have visited with him all day. We were interrupted when I heard someone from across the street yelling my name. I noticed Truman motioning for me to come over. As I turned to join him, I bid Jake goodbye, and told him how much I enjoyed our visit. Jake replied, "We will have many more visits." Little did I realize then, but my friendship with this man would result in the most valuable and enlightening experiences of my life. Jake and his words of wisdom would greatly impact my future.

When I reached Truman, he said, "I see you and Jake have hit it off." I told Truman that Jake was one of the most fascinating men I had ever met. He nodded in agreement, and said Jake was as much a part of Towaoc as the Sleeping Ute Mountain. Then changing the subject, Truman said there should be some copies of previous budgets in the file cabinets in my office, if I could find them. He asked me to go over some of them and work up a new budget to submit at the next Council meeting. I told him that I would take care of it.

Even though I had planned to spend the day gathering contact information and visiting with the business owners, I was glad Truman had asked me to review the past budgets. I was interested in just how much had been allocated to run the security on the reservation. I also wanted to determine just how often the three security patrol cars were replaced. But equally as important, I wanted to see if there was a way to work in a salary position for Jim.

I was happy to find I was able to meet with most of the business owners. I was especially impressed when I met Mr. Ben Hogan, the man in charge of the youth activity center, officially called the "Ute Mountain Youth Activity Center." It was a large building and contained a nice, hardwood basketball court, a large pool, and various activity rooms. It seemed to be the main gathering spot for young people on the reservation. This was indeed where my brother, Fred, refereed basketball games.

After returning to the office, I hung around until Paul showed up. Paul asked me how things were going, and I told him that I had put all these business reports in a new file cabinet, explaining when these business reports were all complete and up to date, we would need to get a copy of them to the Montezuma County Sheriff's dispatcher. That way, if an alarm or a call came in on any of the businesses, the dispatcher could contact the storeowner immediately and have them meet us there.

When I arrived at home, I found Belinda to be in a great mood. The movers had arrived early that morning and had put all the furniture exactly where she wanted. She and Betty had spent the entire day unpacking. They had done an incredible job making our new house look and feel like a home.

Belinda told me to go sit down and relax and dinner would be ready shortly. I walked out on the deck. Again, another beautiful sunset framed the Sleeping Ute. After a few minutes, my wife joined me. I gathered her in my arms and thanked her for allowing this new life to unfold. I was feeling excited about our new adventure and hopeful about the good things I could do for the people of the Ute Mountain Ute Tribe Reservation.

Turns out I wasn't going to have to wait long before getting started on those good things. Shortly after falling asleep, I was awakened by a telephone call. It was Paul. He told me he had just received a call from the county dispatcher advising him of a disturbance involving gunfire. Another call was beeping on the line, so I asked Paul to hold on. It was a dispatcher from the Montezuma County Sheriff's Department who informed me of the same thing. The address of the disturbance was on Sand Circle. I told Paul I would be there in 20 minutes and to wait outside of the residence until I arrived.

With Belinda's help I slipped on a jacket. I promised I'd be in contact. When she saw me take my off duty pistol her face said it all. Part of the reason she was so supportive of my new job was my assurance that I most likely wouldn't need to carry a firearm. I told her not to worry, I had a deputy on duty that carried a gun, and my off-duty pistol was just a precaution.

On the way, I called the Montezuma County Sheriff's dispatcher and advised them I was en route. I also told them not to send any Sheriff's officers unless I asked for them.

When I arrived at the scene, I found Paul was already there. I asked him if he had heard any more shots. He said there had not been any since he arrived. Together, we approached the residence. About 20 feet from the front door, we bumped into a chain link fence. As I reached down to unlatch the gate, we were met by a very large German Shepherd barking viciously. As it stood on its hind feet, its head was almost as high as mine. I knew it could come over the fence if it wanted to.

A small, young woman on the front porch yelled, "Dog!" She clapped her hands and ordered the dog to go to its doghouse. The dog quickly left and went to the back of the house. I thanked her and asked if we could enter the yard. She responded, "Sure," motioning us to come up on the porch.

The porch was better lit, and I instantly recognized the woman as Vonna, the waitress from Merna's. I greeted her and asked her whether she knew my deputy, Paul Wolf. She said that she knew Paul, his brother Jay, and their friend Pinky. I was somewhat puzzled by the emphasis she put on the name Pinky.

Vonna invited us to come in and asked what she could do for us. I explained we had been called by the Sheriff's dispatcher to investigate a disturbance, and that gunfire had been heard. Looking annoyed, Vonna quipped, "I wonder which one of my nosy neighbors called." I told her they probably became alarmed and even concerned for her safety after they heard gunshots.

Vonna motioned for us to sit down without responding. Looking at me, Vonna said that only one shot had been fired and that she thought she had hit him in the butt. I immediately asked Vonna who "him" was. She said she would rather not say, as he was married.

I noticed that after she said he was married, she glanced in Paul's direction and looked at him strangely. She told us she had recently ended an affair with this person, and he had showed up drunk and had forced his way into her house. I replied that I was surprised the person had been able to get past her dog. She commented that the dog knew him and wouldn't attack him.

I learned that Vonna's last name was Kanopi and she was 23. She said she didn't want to kill the person, but rather scare him and make him stay away. I asked her if I could see the gun. She went into another room and returned carrying a small 22 caliber revolver. She informed us all it had in it were 22 shorts. Shorts would inflict the least amount of injury to a person but could still hurt them or even kill them.

Paul, who had been sitting on Vonna's sofa, remained quiet during the interview. He finally spoke up and asked me if he could see the weapon. Replying, "Of course," I handed the weapon to him. Somehow, by the way Paul examined the gun and his quietness, I got the impression that he knew something about this case he wasn't sharing with me.

Upon examining the gun, I found only four chambers were loaded. Vonna must have fired two shots. Turning to her, I asked her how many times she struck him, and she replied, "Only once." I ask her how she explained two empty chambers. She said she fired a warning shot first. I told her and Paul that I would notify the local hospitals and alert them to watch for a gunshot wound to the backside. I told Vonna that I would have to make a report about the incident, and I would need to take her gun and hold on to it. I explained to her that if nobody showed up at any of the local hospitals or didn't make a report of the incident anywhere else, that I would return the handgun to her.

As Paul and I departed, she called out to me, saying that she liked me and the way I had treated her. She then said something that I didn't understand at all. She said that I might be the one Jake had been looking for and telling everyone about. Confused by her parting comment, I waved to her and told her not to hesitate to call us if she needed help again, especially if the man returned. Paul spoke up then and said, "He's not going to return."

I told Paul that I would complete the incident report and contact the hospitals from home. All too many times in the past, I had worried Belinda with similar calls, and I knew she would be waiting up. So, I started home. But instead of thinking about the actual disturbance, I found myself pondering Vonna's unusual comment about me being the one Jake had been looking for.

When I arrived home, the lights were on. I hurried inside and gave my wife a hug and thanked her for waiting up. I assured her that it was not a dangerous call, and I never touched my firearm. I further assured her that the calls on the reservation would never be as bad as the calls in Wichita.

My wife seemed to be more at ease now that I was home, and she fell asleep telling me about some minor adjustments she planned to make to our home and some new furniture she wanted to buy. While I laid next her, I found it impossible to turn my thoughts off. I found myself thinking about Jake and how much I was looking forward to visiting with him again.

The next morning, I awoke to an absolutely beautiful day. I felt drawn to our deck. A glance toward the Sleeping Ute showed that other than a few clouds over his chest, it was a clear day. After a relaxing breakfast with Belinda, I started toward the reservation.

On my drive to work, I thought about the many things I needed to do that day. I knew I had to go to Brick's in Cortez to get my uniform shirts. I also wanted to pick up a few other things for the office. As I continued down the highway, I couldn't help but notice how the Sleeping Ute was decorated with intriguing shadows created by the clouds.

When I arrived at the office, I was again struck with how the place needed a thorough cleaning along with a lot of organization. This strengthened my resolve to get Jim hired.

Pinky was working Jay's late shift, as this was one of Jay's days off. I told Pinky that as soon as they all got used to their new schedules and sleep habits, I wanted to have a meeting with them to discuss what they thought about hiring someone to clean up the office and run errands for us. Of course, the Council would have to determine whether their budget would allow it before approving the hire.

Pinky commented that he thought that was a good idea and that he had a couple of people in mind for the job. I didn't tell him I already had the perfect candidate. Just before Pinky left, he ran over and grabbed a pillow from one of the chairs and walked out the door. I noticed that as he walked, he had somewhat of a limp to his gait, too. I thought back to last night's shooting incident at Vonna's. I was hoping Pinky's sore backside was just a coincidence. I also remembered how strange Paul had acted. I decided to get into that later, or possibly not at all. Had Vonna been more upset, Pinky and I would be having a serious discussion.

As I watched Pinky hobble away, I noticed Jake had taken up his position across the street. The blanket he had draped over his shoulders on this day was deep azure blue.

I decided to walk over to visit with Jake before checking in with some of the business owners. Merna's didn't have too large of a crowd yet, but by the smell of things the diner would be packed soon. Autry's didn't seem to be open yet. As I reached Jake, I told him that it was a lot cooler in the mornings now and that he may have to move his office inside. That drew a big smile. I had never observed Jake standing, but I assumed him to be about 5'6" or 5'7". He had a very slender frame. As I stood there looking into his face, I was captivated by the understanding and kindness in his eyes. His face was weathered and lined, but he somehow managed to emit an aura of youth and vitality.

Jake said some afternoon, before it got much colder, he'd like me to accompany him to a sacred site on the Sleeping Ute Mountain, pointing toward the part of the mountain that formed the Great Warrior's arm folded over his chest. I asked if I was allowed to go up there. He said I could as long he accompanied me.

I took him up on his offer and told him I looked forward to it. Jake continued, saying he would show me things from the past that would help me understand more about his people. He then said, "You know Robert, it is only by staying connected with our past, that we really discover what our pathway in this life is. When we reach the sacred grounds on the Sleeping Ute, I will share with you some of the truths about this life, truths that might make your purpose here in Towaoc clearer."

Jake said he made this journey several times a year, and that I was the only one he had ever asked to accompany him. I felt honored, but still didn't know why Jake wanted me to go with him. He went on to say that this was his way of staying close to the Great Spirit and learning more about his people and all humanity. "We know no more of our fellow man than we do of the Great Spirit," he continued, looking at me more seriously. He then asked if that made any sense to me. And while I didn't fully understand what Jake was saying, I responded I had a pretty good idea what he was getting at.

He then said he wanted to share a few of his thoughts about religion and Christianity. He explained that the Bible was the Christian book of faith. It was interpreted many ways, and that was why we had so many different denominations and faiths. The Torah was the holy scriptures for the Jewish faith. In fact, every world religion had a name for their higher power and some form of a "guidebook." But most of the world religions had two things in common: They all believed in a higher power; and they all believed there was some form of life or consciousness after death. Looking at me, Jake said, "So you see Robert, the people of the world have more in common than they think.

As Jake sat back in his chair, he told me to think upon these things. He then asked me to set a time and date when I could accompany him to the sacred grounds and connect with the Great Spirit on the mountain. He said, "I am hoping you will gain a greater understanding about life, thus adding to your inner strength."

Jake then made a profound statement, which I would never forget. Looking up at the sky, he said, "Always remember, as this is the most important thing, I will ever say to you: the good that you do and have within you is the only true power you will ever possess."

Jake and I agreed to make this journey the following Saturday, at 11 a.m., weather permitting. Then with a big smile, Jake asked me if my wife was a good cook. "Of course," I replied. Jake responded, "Great. Maybe she could prepare a picnic lunch for us, as it will be about lunchtime when we arrive at our destination." He also said he thought we should borrow Pinky's Jeep, as my patrol car would have a hard time making the trip. I didn't know Pinky had a Jeep, but I assured him I would ask.

I regretted leaving Jake, but I did after all have a job to do. I spent the rest of the day visiting with the store owners and going through the files in the office trying to get them in some sort of order. I left a little early so I could drive to Cortez and get fitted for my uniforms.

The following three days, I was busy repairing my car radio and organizing the office. The weather remained pleasant for September. It was cold in the mornings, but usually warmed up during the day. Pinky told me that I could use his Jeep anytime, I would just need to put some gas in it. He also let me know his Jeep was equipped with a communication radio.

As I left the reservation Friday evening, I glanced in my rearview mirror several times as the sun was setting outlining the Sleeping Ute with a silvery glow. Each time I looked, the silvery color changed, turning into a pale yellow and then into a shimmering gold. I couldn't help thinking about my upcoming journey tomorrow with Jake and what the day would reveal.

Belinda was working in the front yard when I arrived home. She wanted to know if our adventure was still on for tomorrow. I assured her it was. She said she would send us chicken salad sandwiches and some peanut butter bars for dessert. I thanked her and asked her to send a thermos of coffee along with some water in case Jake was not a coffee drinker.

As I lay in bed that night, I reflected on all that was happening. It was hard to believe within just a few weeks I'd secured a new career, bought and furnished a new home with my wife, and was laying the foundation of becoming what I hoped to be a valuable member of the Towaoc community. Most of my thoughts, however, were on Jake. I had never met anyone like him. His words and wisdom seemed to reveal the treasures of life. I could hardly wait for our trip tomorrow.

After breakfast with Belinda, I gathered what I needed for the day. Along with the picnic lunch Belinda made I grabbed one of our coffee makers to take to the office. After a kiss goodbye, I was on my way. My first stop was a donut shop I'd noticed along my drive to work.

I entered the donut shop and a middle-aged man in an apron approached me. I told him to pick out a dozen assorted donuts for me. As he was filling my order, I told him I didn't see any name on his shop, other than "donuts." He first introduced himself as Zeke, and then proceeded to tell me with a smile that he felt "donuts" got right to it. No one would wonder what he was selling." I told him I would have to agree, it takes the mystery out of things. He continued saying it seems to be working because business is good, so good in fact that he was thinking of opening another shop, this one would offer a more extensive bakery menu and he would offer delivery services to the local businesses. "That's a terrific idea, Zeke," I said. "My name is Robert Brown and I'm the new Chief of Security. These donuts right here are for my deputies. I can guarantee you; we would be among your best customers." He laughed handing me the box of donuts saying, "Looking forward to that Robert. Have a great day. It looks like the Great Spirit is giving us blue skies and golden sunshine today." Nodding in agreement, I turned and walked into those beautiful weather conditions Zeke just described thinking to myself, "it is going to be great day."

Pinky was on the phone when I got to the station. I noticed he hadn't strayed far from his trusty pillow. Smiling when he saw the coffee pot and box of donuts, he got up and took both off my hands.

Pinky remembered I needed his Jeep. He said I should probably gas it up before I go and asked if I could run him by his house on my way out. Pinky had already gotten into the box of donuts and was eating a chocolate covered one. He said if I didn't care he would take another one and it would be his breakfast. I told him that's my kind of breakfast and to help himself.

As we got into Pinky's Jeep, Pinky put his pillow in the seat before he sat down. I didn't say anything. As I drove toward his house, I noticed the gas gauge was on empty. I asked Pinky if we had enough gas to make it. He assured me that there should be two gallons left. After I let him off, I headed straight for a gas station near the edge of the highway and filled the tank.

When I arrived back at the office, I read Pinky's report about the night's activity. The report simply stated that two people had come in complaining about Vonna's dog barking. Not one mention of gunshots. I figured I would just leave this between Pinky and his pillow.

Chapter 6

"Glimpses"

Even though we had planned to leave around 11 a.m., considering the beautiful day, and quiet peaceful state of things, Jake and I decided to hit the road early. So, at 9:30 a.m. I loaded Pinky's Jeep with our lunch and supplies. I then contacted the dispatcher and informed them that for the next several hours I'd be reachable by the Jeep's radio. Jake chose a soft green blanket for our journey. As we headed out, he told me to prepare for a strong feeling of peace when we reached the place where the Great Warrior slept. He said his whole purpose for taking me up to visit such a sacred place was to enhance and bring out what goodness I possessed "Robert, the only power or strength you will ever have in this life, will come from your inner thoughts." What Jake had just said to me sounded somewhat reasonable, I couldn't argue or disagree with him. I did not, however, fully understand it. I had always thought of power as pertaining to my physical ability, and powerful positions of authority. I thought Jake, however, was talking about a different source of power.

I told him to lead the way. Little did I know at the time, but I was about to embark on a journey that would change my whole perception of life, and the way I viewed my fellowman. I would not return the same person.

After we were out of town, Jake pointed to a dirt road, which seemed to be going in the direction of the Great Warrior's knee. Pinky's Jeep was pretty noisy, so it was hard to visit while we were on the road. We must have traveled 10 miles when Jake waved to get my attention and pointed to the north.

I turned onto what must have been a bike trail and headed northwest, thinking how grateful I was that it hadn't rained recently.

It was almost 11:00 a.m., our original time of departure. We had covered quite a distance, though I couldn't drive much over 10 miles per hour. Another reason I was glad we left early. We continued in this direction for quite some time. I observed that several small clouds were now forming over our destination. The clouds resembled a blanket pulled up to the Great Warrior's chest. Jake motioned for me to pull over and stop.

After I came to a stop, Jake told me that many Ute elders believed the clouds held rain, and that the Great Warrior would gather them up, usually by noon, and put them in his pockets. Then, if he was happy with his people, he would let the clouds slip out of his pockets and provide rain. He was surprised to learn that I had already knew of this Ute legend. Jake then motioned for me to drive forward, heading in the same direction.

By this time, we started ascending the mountain. Until this point, we had traveled through barren desert land. Now we were amid fragrant ponderosa pines and white-barked aspens. Jake told me to pull over and stop, saying we'd arrived. Once I turned the engine off, I was struck by the silence. Then suddenly a blast of wind interrupted the stillness, stirring up leaves in a swirl around us.

The clouds had vanished, and the sun was shining brightly. Perhaps the Great Warrior gathered them and stuffed them into his pockets. I was struck again by how peaceful it was, the stillness only occasionally broken with bird song. A great sense of peace came over me and I found myself thinking how happy I was to be alive and here with Jake in such an ancient and sacred place. I was basking in tranquility, when Jake broke the trance I was in. He asked me where our lunch was. Glancing at my watch, I saw it was already lunchtime. I retrieved our lunches from Pinky's Jeep along with a large blanket and followed Jake over to a level spot. I spread the blanket out and put our lunches on it. I asked Jake if he wanted coffee or water. Jake replied, "Coffee, please, no cream or sugar." After eating a bite of his chicken salad sandwich and taking a big drink of coffee, he leaned back on one elbow and said, "Isn't this great, Robert?" My mouth full, I could merely nod enthusiastically in agreement.

After breaking bread together, Jake said, "My ancestors believed all life is sacred and that all of mankind is intertwined and connected." Jake continued, "What you need to do, Robert - what we all need to do - is transform our good and true beliefs into good and true deeds and actions. When you do that, you form meaningful connections with people and bring a bit of heaven down to Earth."

Motioning around him, Jake said, "If there is one Divine power and that one Divine power is the creator of us all, how could people ever hate or destroy each other? It would almost be like us trying to destroy the Divine power." "Which is impossible."

Continuing to look at me as he talked, Jake said the reason the European people prevailed so easily against the American Indian nations was because of the American Indian people's beliefs. "Primarily the one that I just mentioned, Robert. They believed if you hated or tried to kill what the Great Sprit had created, you were in effect trying to destroy the Great Spirit." Jake continued, "It wasn't until our ancestors began to wage destruction on a large scale that violence and disease crept into their lives. When your thoughts are filled with love and compassion, they manifest in good health and happiness. But when your mind is filled with hate and revenge, those thoughts manifest in sickness and disease."

Jake then looked at me with a big smile and said, "You know, Robert, from an early age, American Indian children are taught to love all living things. Sometimes, while growing up, if they are particularly fond of a certain animal, they are given its name as their second name. We feel all living things are related because they are all born from the same source." He continued saying, "We should all have a goal in this life, and part of that goal should be to discover our purpose here on earth. The other part of that goal should be to fulfill that purpose." Pausing for a moment and looking at me, Jake asked, "Robert, do you understand what your purpose in life is?"

Before I had a chance to answer, he continued, saying we all reflect the Great Spirit, Allah, or God, or however we refer to the Divine power, in our own special way, and have our own special purpose in life, which no other person could fulfill. "Robert", Jake said, "It is important for you to know what your purpose is. Because only you can fulfill it." So, you see, we are each very important. Our purpose unfolds daily. And with each day, we grow in our understanding. Our understanding will continue to grow until we see our purpose. Then, we will also see the Divine power. Of course, Robert, I don't mean to "see" literally. I am speaking of a spiritual understanding."

He gave that a minute to sink in before saying, "Robert, you experience positive spiritual energy by focusing your attention on what is good and loving. Where your thoughts are, so is your heart, and that's where your energy flows. My whole reason for bringing you up on this mountain with me is to help you discover your purpose in life."

Jake was almost nonstop talk now. I didn't mind, as everything he said fascinated me. Some of it I didn't fully grasp, however what he was saying wasn't too far removed from what in my heart I've always believed. Doing good, attracts good and we are all more closely connected that we realize.

"For you Robert and for our conversations I will refer to the Divine power as God. As that is what you are most accustomed to. But know this Divine power will answer us no matter what name we call. We are limited in our understanding of ourselves, and how well we understand this supreme power. We can know no more of each other, then we know of it. You can't understand a reflection until you understand the object of the reflection."

By then it was almost 2:00 p.m. I had completely lost track of time. Rolling over on the blanket and looking up at the blue sky, I commented to Jake that I was tired. It wasn't so much a physical tiredness, as a mental one.

Looking at me, Jake commented that I needed some "spiritual energy." He told me that I would get this energy by focusing my attention and thoughts in the right direction, concentrating on how much good I could accomplish. He then told me that if I wanted to be successful as the new Security Chief, I had to concentrate on making the reservation a positive place. "Don't forget, Robert, where your thoughts are, so is your heart, and that is where your energy flows. That is why it is so important to entertain thoughts of love and goodwill."

"What I want you to try to do, Robert, is close your eyes and completely relax." When you are completely calm, attempt to recall a pleasant place you have visited or possibly where you come from. This can be a home you loved, a park, a lake, or any place that was or is especially dear to you."

After a few minutes of silence, Jake softly asked if I had a place in mind. I did. I was thinking of the back patio of my family's first home in Wichita, Kansas. I was trying to recall the different trees, and the way the backyard looked with my son's tree house and my daughter's playhouse, and the children running and playing there. Jake then instructed me to focus intently on one specific quality or feature. I was drawn to a huge oak tree in the backyard with ornamental rock surrounding its base. He asked if I could see what I was concentrating on clearly, and I said yes. After a few seconds, he asked me to return my thoughts to where we were on the mountain and open my eyes.

Jake then asked me where I'd been. I replied that I was recalling my backyard and patio at my home in Wichita. Jake then asked me if I had been there. I replied that I had been there only in my thoughts. Jake then asked me again, "you were there then, weren't you?" Again, I responded that it was only in my thoughts.

"That's all for now, Robert. I want you to think back on what we discussed today. Someday, humankind may discover they don't need cars, boats, or airplanes to get from one place to another. Someday, after going through many phases of spiritual development, they may awake to the fact that they are becoming less flesh and more spirit. That would mean becoming less human and more spiritual, and more connected to God.

Looking at his watch for the first time, Jake said, "It's getting late, perhaps we should start back." As I was gathering up our things, I observed Jake looking around where we had been sitting. I noticed him staring at some things for long time. Then, looking at me, he said, "I'm trying to get a good mental picture of this place, Robert. I may want to return."

Jake was quiet on the way back, only speaking when I needed to make a turn. After we arrived Towaoc, I asked Jake where he wanted me to drop him off. Pointing in the direction of his chair, he said, "Right there will do." I told him I had really enjoyed our journey. Looking at me, Jake smiled and replied, "We will go back. I wanted you to see you could experience the past and the present at the same time in your mind. I think you understand somewhat how you can mentally be somewhere else by recalling the past. What you must do, what we must all do, is learn how to mentally be not only in the present, but in the future."

As he got out and shut the door, he looked at me with warmth in his eyes and asked, "How long have you been God's reflection? Was there ever a time where when you did not reflect God? Do you think there will ever be a time when you do not reflect God? Think on these things, Robert."

I felt completely at ease as I drove home. It was almost as if the spiritual thoughts Jake and I had shared that day had satiated my human appetite to the point of complete satisfaction

When I arrived home, my wife seemed in an unusually good mood. I knew from her expression she must have gone shopping, one her favorite pastimes. She asked me to join her on the deck for the sunset. The Sleeping Ute was draped in a blanket of clouds, glowing with silver and gold. We watched the shifting colors until they were swallowed by the night.

The next two weeks went by without any incidents. I concentrated on getting the office records and paperwork in order. I also got my uniform shirts and was able to get the police radios in all our cars transferred to their own channels. We were all making good use of the coffee maker and I was bringing in Zeke's donuts on a pretty regular basis.

I am thinking about Jim working at the office when I received a call from the head of the Bureau of Indian Affairs in Washington, D.C., a gentleman by the name of Mr. Ben Townsend. Mr. Townsend was concerned with obtaining an update on the state of affairs of the Ute Mountain Ute Tribe Reservation. He wanted some figures regarding how many of its citizens were unemployed.

I assured Mr. Townsend that at the Council meeting next week I would get some figures for him. In addition to our regular government aid, which I knew nothing about at that time, he felt the reservation would be entitled to some additional assistance for job training, food stamps, and unemployment compensation. He also assured me now, with the winter months ahead, that warm blankets and clothing would be coming. After our talk, I asked Pinky how I could get the key to the Bureau of Indian Affairs building. Pinky said Truman had the key.

This was great news for the reservation, so I wanted to start gathering the information Mr. Townsend requested immediately. I was able to obtain the office key from Truman and got to work going through many books and documents.

I brought the most important and recent books and paperwork home with me, so I could ensure I had everything together for the next Council meeting. One thing was evident as I read through everything: the Ute Mountain Ute Tribe Reservation, as well as all the reservations, were each a separate and sovereign nation.

I learned that our government had made some treaties with the reservation in the late 1800s and early 1900s that forbid the settling of any land by American citizens within 50 miles of the reservation. Some of these treaties were made and signed by President Teddy Roosevelt and stated that each reservation had sole authority and governing responsibility of its people. I guessed that this was the reason for the Council members and head Council member, Truman House. They were, in fact, the complete governing body of this reservation.

The puzzling part, however, was a document that stated the 50-mile buffer zone surrounding the reservation was off limits to developers. The town of Cortez was only 12 miles away. I searched through some of the other volumes and couldn't find any treaties overriding or changing this stipulation. I decided I would have a local attorney take a look at this document.

During the next several days, there were times I felt perhaps I should drop it because I might just stir up trouble. These thoughts were quickly replaced, however, with a desire to help the people on the reservation obtain all their rights. I felt Jake would agree.

Chapter 7

"Human Footsteps"

It's hard to describe the motivating force I felt after visiting the sacred place on the Sleeping Ute. In some way, I was feeling a connection with the spiritual or the Divine. Jake said that this connection would come when I had a constant sensation of love. I suppose my drive to make things better for the residents of the reservation was in fact a sensation of love.

While going through the volumes the night after returning from my trip with Jake, I received a message on my pager. It only said, "Disturbance, report immediately."

When I got to town, I noticed Pinky's car and a crowd outside of Autry's. Pinky approached me and said he had called an ambulance as a man was hurt and bleeding.

People on the sidewalk were trying to help the injured man. I quickly learned that my old friend from Wichita, Jim Goodriver, was involved in this disturbance. Pinky said that he was holding another man inside. I also learned that Bill was inside trying to talk to him.

I entered the front door of Autry's and saw Jim standing over a man crouched on his hands and knees. I called over to Jim and told him it was Brown. Bill was standing nearby looking terrified. I told Bill that everything was going to be all right.

The fellow on his hands and knees didn't seem to be injured; I thought he was just afraid to stand up.

I asked Jim to accompany me to the bar area. Jim was hesitant. I said I wanted to help him get this resolved before the Sheriff's deputies were called. This got his attention. I gently guided him over to the bar and told him I needed to check on the injured man out front.

Stepping outside, I saw one of the ambulance drivers attending to a man sitting on the edge of the curb. The other man, the one who had just left the bar, was talking to Pinky. I asked the ambulance driver if the man was hurt bad. He advised me that the one talking to Pinky was just bruised, but the other one had some cuts and was bleeding, and he felt he needed to go to the hospital to get stitches. Reaching out, I shook his hand and identified myself, as I was not in uniform. I told him to advise the hospital officials I would be there in about 30 minutes and not to release the injured man until I got there.

I asked Pinky how the other man was. He replied he was just bruised and sore. Both men were American Indians, and I assumed they were both residents of the reservation. I asked Pinky to take a report from the man, and that I was going back to talk to Jim and Bill. As I entered Autry's, I found that Jim was helping Bill sweep up some broken glass on the floor. I told Bill we would cover any damages and asked Jim to join me out in my car, as I wanted to talk to him.

As we left Autry's, the ambulance was pulling away. They weren't using red light or sirens, a good sign that the man's injuries were not serious.

I told Pinky not to worry about the paperwork on this, that I would take care of it and go by the hospital to follow up on the injured man. I told Jim to get in my car and I would give him a ride home. I winked at him and said, "You can even ride shot gun." That got a small smile out him. Jim got in but told me he didn't know whether he could go back to his brother's or not.

While we sat in the car, Jim told me his side of the story, claiming his brother's wife had started it all. He said she had come home from work that evening angry with him, telling him she was not going to work hard all day at the cleaners in Cortez and come home to Jim, who just laid around, and feed him. Jim said he yelled some not so nice things at her, slammed the door and ended up at Autry's.

Jim further explained that the two men he got in the fight with were talking about him at the bar. He said he overheard one of them refer to him as a "big dumb" Indian. Looking at me real serious, he said he was not going to let anyone talk about him like that, and especially when he was already in a bad mood.

Looking Jim right in the eye, I said, "Jim, if you do me a favor, I'll do you one." Jim replied it depended on what I wanted. I told Jim the next time he feels angry in a situation try taking some deep breaths and counting to 10, or taking a walk, anything to avoid lashing out. "Jim," I pleaded, "don't get in anymore fights or trouble." I told him I would have to take a report from the man he'd injured, and there was a chance that if he pressed charges, I would have to put Jim in jail. I assured him I'd do everything to make sure that didn't happen, but if something like this happened again, there would only be so much I could do.

I then told Jim what my favor was. If he tried to control his anger, starting next Monday, he had a steady job cleaning the office and running errands. That is, if I could convince the man he attacked not to press charges. Again, I told him I was confident I could work things out. I explained that having a steady job would make his brother's wife happy. Knowing he was worried about returning to his brother's home I told him

I would come in with him and tell his brother's wife about his new job. Jim gave me a faint smile and told me I had a deal.

When I pulled up in front of Jim's brother's house, Jim said in almost a whisper, "I'll bet Olivia thinks the police are coming with that big dumb brother." I assured Jim it was going to be alright.

Olivia met us at the front door. I introduced myself and told her I had given Jim a ride home. I also explained that Jim was going to work for me, and that I was going to count on him to straighten up my office and keep things running smoothly, sort of like an office manager. Maybe it was the importance I hinted about Jim helping me, or the spur of the moment title I'd given him, but Olivia just stood and stared at Jim and me. She finally broke the silence by congratulating Jim on finding such an important job and telling him that his brother would sure be proud.

I told Jim to come to the office Monday at 10 a.m. While I had yet to present hiring Jim to the Council, circumstances warranted I act immediately. The Council meeting was Monday and I felt confident I would be supported in my appointment of Jim.

Looking up the street, I saw the crowd had left Autry's. As a matter of fact, the streets were deserted except for Jake, wrapped in a silvery grey blanket. He waved. I waved back in return. I desperately wanted to tell him what happened, but I knew it had been several hours and my wife would be worried. So, I headed for home.

Pulling off the reservation and onto the highway, I glanced in my rearview mirror – a now comforting ritual - at the Sleeping Ute and had the strangest feeling the Great Warrior was watching me. I found my thoughts flooded with all I had learned from the many volumes concerning the Bureau of

Indian Affairs and the possible violation of the rights of the people of the reservation.

Early the next morning I headed to the hospital to speak with the man who had the confrontation with Jim. It was my hope I could convince him not to press charges. If I couldn't, my plan to have Jim work for me would go right out the window.

At the hospital I found that the man's injuries were minor. I told him by not pressing charges against Jim he could keep his pride from being injured as well. "After all, I said, "do you really want to acknowledge you were outdone by some 'big dumb' Indian." The man required no further convincing.

On my way home, I felt compelled to drive to Cortez. I found myself pulling over and parking near the shop where I had gotten my uniforms.

The building I parked in front of had gold lettering on the front window that read, "Randall Beaver & Son, Attorneys at Law." When I got out of my car, I felt a sudden blast of wind. I once again began thinking about those volumes regarding the Bureau of Indian Affairs. I found myself walking up to the front door of the attorney's office building.

Inside, I was greeted by a woman who appeared to be of American Indian descent, probably as much or more so than me. I introduced myself and explained that I was the new Security Chief for the Mountain Ute Tribe Reservation, and also head of the Bureau of Indian Affairs for the reservation.

I told her I wanted to consult with an attorney regarding some of the legal language in the volumes I was reading. As if on cue, a man in a suit, about my age, emerged from one of the interior offices. The woman announced, "This is my father-in-law, Randy Beaver." He owns the law firm. He had his hand extended and I reached out and shook it and introduced myself.

I explained to Mr. Beaver that when I took the job to head up security on the reservation, I also inherited the job as head of the Bureau of Indian Affairs. I told him that I had been going through many volumes in the office, and I needed some help interpretating the legalese, in particular I needed clarity around language concerning a 50-mile buffer zone around the Ute Mountain Ute Tribe Reservation.

Mr. Beaver responded that he would be happy to look them over for me and give his opinion on whatever I was unsure of. I replied that I did not have the volumes with me and requested as to what time his office opened on Monday, given this was Friday.

He replied with a smile that his office would open at 9:00 a.m. on Monday. I told him I'd see him then. When I got back to my car, I noticed the Sleeping Ute. Even though it was nearly dark, I could still make out the silhouette form. I felt a deep sense of calm, yet I felt invigorated at the same time. Jake told me on our journey to the sacred land on the Sleeping Ute Mountain, that one can find spiritual energy in doing good for others. Could this surge of energy be a result of what I just did? And, if that's the case I was really liking how good doing good things felt.

I decided to head home and get a jump start on the weekend. My wife and I enjoyed a leisurely dinner and talked about our daughter's recent move to Richmond, Virginia and looked at the photographs my daughter sent of our two precious granddaughters. I found myself pondering the fact that children seem to have a deeper appreciation of life than adults. They have a sense of innocence and wonder that I wish didn't fade as we grew older. It made me reflect on how to keep that youthful spirit alive, which of course made me think of Jake. Yes, Jake had figured it out. Now it's my turn.

Over the weekend I completed reading all the volumes I brought home. I needed Mr. Beaver to interpret just what the buffer zone was, and the clause that stated that the government was responsible for any infringements on the reservation and could be held monetarily responsible. I was trying to understand if this meant the government would have to pay the people living on the reservation, because I was unable to find anything in the later volumes where the government had ever made any agreements with any governing Councils, or that anyone had purchased the buffer zone.

In fact, I was unable to find anything in any of the volumes where any change had been made to the wording in the earliest volumes. I did conclude however that with the importance riding on this interpretation, I would bring all the volumes I had to Mr. Beaver's office.

I was up early Monday morning. There was a lot to accomplish in an hour. First, I needed to give Mr. Beaver all the volumes and make sure he understood what he needed to do. Then, I needed to prepare Pinky, Jay, and Paul for Jim's arrival.

I arrived at Mr. Beaver's office about 15 minutes before nine. I was happy to find the receptionist was already opening the office. I brought all eight volumes inside and deposited them on the front desk. She informed me that Mr. Beaver was expecting me. I was so thankful these folks were punctual. I lost no time in telling him where I needed his legal expertise. He assured me that he would go through all of them.

In no time, I found myself pulling onto the reservation. In less than an hour I would be going to my first Council meeting. I hurried toward the office hoping I'd beat Jim there. Turns out, Jim wanted to make sure he was early for his first day of work. Pinky and Jay burst through the front door. Pinky was looking over his shoulder saying something I couldn't make out. When Jay reached down to release the safety strap covering his sidearm, I shouted to them, asking what was going on. Jay yelled back, "It's that crazy fool, Jim!" Pinky chimed in and said Jim had just thrown the door open and walked in on them. I asked

Pinky and Jay if anyone had been hurt or anything else had happened. Jay replied, "No, he just busted in on us."

Jim stood in the doorway. He almost filled the whole frame. I had reached Pinky and Jay by this time and put my hand on Jay's shoulder saying, "Guys, this whole thing is my fault. I was supposed to tell you before this morning. I'm the one who asked Jim to come by. I have some work around the office Jim can do for us."

Meanwhile, I called out to Jim, who was still standing in the front doorway, and told him that everything was fine, and that Pinky and Jay just weren't expecting any visitors. I told him to go wait inside and we'd be there in a minute.

I turned to my frazzled and confused deputies and explained that the work I had in mind for Jim would keep him busy and out of trouble which would reduce the chance of us getting hurt breaking up his disturbances. I also told them, if it didn't work out, I'd let him go.

This seemed to satisfy them. As we walked back into the office, I told them that I was going to show Jim how to make a really great cup of coffee. I also sweetened the pot by promising extra donuts.

Entering the office, I found Jim sitting at my desk. Considering the circumstances, I was glad he'd chosen my desk and not Pinky's or Jay's. I told him that everything was okay and that the whole thing had been my fault. I had failed to tell them that he was coming by to help us. I explained to Jim that he had just startled them. Looking at him with a smile, I asked him, "Wouldn't you be a little startled if someone as big as you suddenly barged in through the front door?" Jim chuckled a little and nodded in agreement.

I then invited everyone to help themselves to a donut. I found myself holding back a smile when Jim chose a pink frosted donut with sprinkles. I then told Jim I was going to share my secret for a great cup of copy. I said you need to measure the coffee, no eyeballing things. Pinky declared, "THAT'S the secret?!" A measuring cup? Give us a break boss!" I answered, "Pinky, often it's the small things that make the biggest difference." Once the coffee is done brewing, you'll see."

Looking at the clock on the wall, it was time to head to the Council meeting. I asked Pinky to show Jim where the push broom was and where the trash bin was in back. "I'm going to run now, guys," and with a smile said, "save me a cup of coffee."

As I walked to the Council building, I felt calm and in control. I remembered Jake telling me that the good we accomplished gave us the only power attainable. Maybe the sense of calm power and peace I was feeling was a result of doing that "good." It was going to be interesting to see what the outcome would be.

As I entered the room where the Council meeting was held, the Council members met me with a greeting almost in unison. It certainly made me feel more relaxed, like I had been fully accepted by the group as one of them. Truman invited me to sit in the chair next to him.

I was impressed with the way the Council meeting was conducted. Each member reported on their specific assignment. The first member, Mr. Hammond reported on the Ute Mountain activity center. He said the floor of the basketball court needed refinishing.

Next, a man by the name of Nick Gunthar reported. He was the grounds man. He gave an update as to the condition of many of the business buildings. Truman then asked him if he had any new information on attracting new businesses to the reservation. This statement aroused my interest. After hearing Mr. Gunthar's explanation, I raised my hand. After Truman acknowledged me, I asked what type of businesses they were looking for. Truman responded by saying any business which would bring employment opportunities. He continued by saying that because the reservation was its own sovereign nation, they didn't have to follow minimum wage guidelines and other work regulations like other towns.

Mr. Gunthar spoke up and said that many of their residents were skilled in wood and metal work and worked as carpenters and machinists in surrounding towns. Looking at me, Truman said that if they could get some local manufacturers to come onto the reservation, that it would improve the people's quality of life and lift the whole community's pride. Nodding my head in agreement, I said I thought it was a wonderful idea, and without thinking asked if they objected to my looking into the possibilities. Truman replied, "Of course not, we'll take all the help we can get."

The Council meeting lasted about two hours. After all the Council members had reported, Truman, looking at me with a smile, asked if I had anything to add. I responded by telling the Council that I did have two things. I very cautiously explained the trouble we recently had with Jim Goodriver. I also asked them if it was within our budget to hire Jim to help in the office and run some errands.

I was watching the expressions on the Council members faces while I talked. With the somewhat negative looks I was seeing, I told them this was at least a way for me to keep an eye on Jim. Still not getting very many positive looks I said, "Just like Truman explained, employment and having more of a sense of purpose can really lift a person up. Having this job could really help Jim." I continued with a smile, "You never know, there could be a time when his size might come in handy."

Finally, I could see some smiles and expressions of "maybe he has a good idea." I offered, "How about we try it for a month." Truman responded by agreeing with me. I thanked Truman and went right on to say they would enjoy hearing about my other matter for discussion more.

The Council member's expressions lit up as I began explaining that after learning one of my responsibilities would be to lead the Bureau of Indian Affairs, I made the decision to go through the Bureau of Indian Affairs volumes. Also, I informed them about the recent phone conversation I had with Mr. Townsend in Washington, D.C.

I explained that in one of the volumes, the oldest one dating back to the early 1800s, I found some early treaties made by our government with the Ute Mountain Indian people, concerning a 50-mile buffer zone surrounding the entire reservation. I further explained that it appeared the neighboring communities had infringed on this buffer zone.

At this point, Mr. Yancey interrupted me asking me what this meant. I replied that I had taken the liberty, and I hoped with their blessing, to have a local attorney look the volumes over and give a legal opinion. Mr. Yancey asked me what, if anything, they could do about it. I replied that we would have to wait for the legal opinion from Mr. Beaver, but to me, it sounded like either the government or the local community should have paid for the buffer zone rights. I further explained that if I was right and they should have been paid for the land, they should not only be compensated starting from when the infringement first happened, but they should receive the interest that money would have earned as well. There was a complete silence over the whole room. One could have heard a pin drop.

I broke the silence, saying that I wouldn't advise repeating this outside of the room or talking amongst themselves about it until we got the legal opinion back from Mr. Beaver. I continued, saying that even if it were a favorable opinion, I would not publish it until the Council decided just what to do with the funds derived from this, and how those funds would be distributed.

Truman spoke up saying I was right and cautioned the other members not to talk about this to anyone, even their families. Truman said that none of them should build up any false hopes until they heard from the attorney. Looking at me, Truman asked me to get in touch with him the minute I heard from Mr. Beaver so he could call a special meeting. Continuing to look around the room, he said that a motion to adjourn the meeting was in order. After hearing one of the members so move and a second, Truman asked all in favor to indicate by saying "Aye," and we adjourned.

As I walked out the front door, I turned and glanced back. I could see that the Council members were all standing out in front of the Council building visiting. I certainly hoped I hadn't raised a lot of false hopes. Then, I felt an arm around my shoulder. Turning slightly, I saw a grinning Truman. He commented how glad he was I had decided to go through those volumes. I responded that I was too.

Heading toward the security office, I glanced over at Suma's Hardware and saw Jake motioning me to come over. When I arrived where he was sitting, I noticed he had an unusually big smile on his face. His rich gold-colored blanket seemed to be a sign of prosperity that would hopefully come to the residents of the reservation. He asked me if the Council meeting had been particularly eventful. He seemed to know, somehow, that something very important had just transpired.

I didn't feel like hiding anything that had been discussed from Jake. As a matter of fact, I felt quite the opposite. So, I told him I had recently discovered some important information in one of the older volumes on Indian Affairs that needed to be interpreted by an attorney. I told him the Council was very much in favor of having the matter investigated.

I had no idea how Jake knew what had been discussed at the Council meeting. His next comment, however, made me wonder. He said, "Robert, if you ever discovered something that would benefit my people with large sums of money, before it is ever made public knowledge, consider the best ways of distribution among the people. It might be that some sort of installments or monthly payments could be worked out."

I was completely taken aback by what Jake was saying. I hope he didn't think me silly, but all I could do was just stand and look at him. I was at a complete loss of words. What this man had just said made complete sense should the government owe these people some money. But how could Jake have known this?

I didn't know whether my mouth was open or not, and I can only imagine the astonished and puzzled look I must have had on my face, but Jake snapped me out of my bewildered state. He asked me if my wife still made those good chicken salad sandwiches. He also commented that he couldn't stop thinking about those peanut butter bars either. He then asked me if I could borrow Pinky's Jeep again and return to visit the Great Warrior on Saturday. I said would love another trip to the Sleeping Ute with him. We set the departure time for 10 a.m.

When I arrived at the office, I found Pinky standing outside looking a bit flustered. He asked what the Council thought about my idea to hire Jim. I told him they thought it might solve our problem of him getting into trouble. I put my arm around Pinky's shoulder and said to him, "Let's give it a try for a week, Pinky." I then told him that I would make a special effort to be around anytime Jim was and would have some more talks with him. This seemed to put Pinky at ease and the rest of the day was pretty routine. I took Jim to Merna's with me for lunch. Jim ate enough for both of us and really seemed to enjoy himself. Other than a few occasional stares, things went really well. Vonna seemed to realize the situation I was in, and

I could tell she was making a special effort to make Jim feel relaxed, keeping his water glass and coffee cup full.

That evening when I returned home, I decided to prepare a list of all the businesses that would benefit the community by being located on the reservation. I reasoned that once the people were trained and felt comfortable in their new jobs, they would be good workers. I didn't want to see people paid a low wage but realized if our proposal to the businesses was to be successful, people may need to accept lower pay than the townspeople to warrant the business coming to the reservation.

My thoughts were led to businesses in the manufacturing category rather than retail chains. I knew that there was a manufactured homes business in Durango. Durango was about 60 miles east of Cortez and was where Jake had obtained one of his degrees. There was also an auto restoration shop in Cortez that painted and detailed cars for some local automobile agencies. I thought it would be worthwhile to take a trip to Durango to discuss the possibility of subcontracting with some of the businesses. I decided to contact them before the next Council meeting.

Belinda interrupted my musings, calling me to come and see the sunset. Joining her, I saw one of the most spectacular sunsets I had ever seen. Over the dark silhouette of the Sleeping Ute body was a light blue outline surrounding him. Hovering over the light blue was a somewhat darker blue outline, and above that was a sky of pink, orange and yellow.

As I stood there taking in the beautiful view, I remembered Jake wanted to visit the Great Warrior again. I turned to my wife and asked if she wouldn't mind making Jake and I another lunch of chicken salad sandwiches on Saturday. I told her how much Jake loved what she'd made, especially the peanut butter bars. She said she would be happy to.

I awoke early the next morning with the feeling that today was a great day to contact some of the businesses I had been considering. I immediately called the office hoping to reach Jay before he left. When he answered, I asked if he wouldn't mind staying a few extra hours for me. Jay graciously agreed and said he hoped Big Jim remembered to bring donuts. I was happy to hear Jay had given Jim a nickname.

The day was quite successful. I was able to contact the owners of the businesses I had considered and found they expressed a lot of interest in moving some of their operations to the reservation. They liked the idea of becoming more connected with the community while also gaining an economic foothold on their competitors. I felt that whatever blessed them would also bless the reservation.

It was nearly noon. I hadn't planned to be gone so long, but everything seemed to have worked out, almost as if by design. As I started for the security office to relieve Jay, I couldn't help but reflect on something Jake told me on our earlier trip to the Sleeping Ute Mountain. When he told me to discover my purpose, I would need to let go of self-doubt and be guided by my inner thoughts. Jake also said our thoughts are all that really exists. Everything else was an illusion. The thoughts that I had were the only thing real about me. I still didn't completely understand this. I suppose it was listening to my inner thoughts that morning that led me to contact the right people, because both owners of the two businesses I called expressed interest and agreed to meet with the Council at their next meeting.

I also wanted this venture to bless these two businesses. Whatever blessed one, had to bless all. My mind wandered back to Jake, who had reassured me that having positive, selfless thoughts will result in good things. He reassured me that all I needed to do to be led and guided by a Divine source was to think positive thoughts and assume positive intent.

When I arrived at the office, I saw Jim already had the coffee on. He had also brought in some of Zeke's donuts. Jay had a donut and cup of coffee in his hand when I walked in. I think he and Jim had just been talking and visiting with each other.

After Jay left, I asked Jim to keep an eye on things for us, as I was going down to visit with Jake. Jim said, "Sure thing Brown" take your time." I couldn't get over how well Jim was working out. And, he had not caused any more trouble at Autry's.

As I stepped out the door, who did I run into, but Jake, wrapped in a deep purple blanket. He was paying me an unexpected and rare visit. I held the door open and invited him in. Jim, who saw Jake walk in, jumped up and pulled out the chair he was sitting in over to my desk. Jim said he was going to walk down to Merna's and see what her special for lunch was. I thanked Jim for his chair and told him not to rush, he had earned a nice break.

As Jake sat down, he commented that he was just dropping in to remind me of our upcoming trip this Saturday. I told Jake I had already turned in our lunch order to my wife. Jake smiled when he heard this. Looking at me somewhat seriously, he asked if I had been busy lately. I knew he was referring to my work involving what I'd discovered in the early volumes from the Bureau of Indian Affairs. I told Jake about the possibility of two local businesses locating on the reservation, giving many of the residents an opportunity for employment as well as health benefits. Jake commented that this would be very good. He said that too often people felt that American Indians could only push brooms or dig ditches, and skilled labor was not for them. Jake said that if these businesses would train his people, they would find that they do very good work.

Then he reached across the desk and placed his hand on my forearm, saying, "Sometimes we lose sight of our spiritual mission. It is not accomplished so much in taking the necessary human footsteps, as it is in seeking and following Divine direction. Sometimes the human mission and spiritual mission go hand in hand." He continued, "Your spiritual mission in life is personal to you, Robert. If you seek this mission with a good and honest heart, and with unselfish thoughts of love, you will be divinely led as to what human footsteps to take. "Remember," Jake said, "how important it is to stay connected. By staying connected you will receive the Divine energy necessary to accomplish whatever it is that you were seeking." Jake then said, "Some people refer to this as Divine inspiration, Robert. But isn't Divine inspiration energy?" I didn't tell Jake, but I guess it was the Divine energy that led me to Mr. Beaver a few days ago.

While I was mid-thought, Jim walked in. Looking over at Jake and me, he announced that Merna's lunch special was fried chicken. I immediately looked over at Jake and asked him if he would like to join Jim and me later at lunchtime. Getting up and turning toward the door, Jake replied with a wink, "I'll pass. I'm having some good chicken tomorrow."

Jim took a seat where Jake had been sitting. The office did look much better. I told Jim how nice I thought the office looked and that he was doing a great job. So good in fact, that as soon as Pinky got in, I would take him to Merna's for her special, my treat.

I had no more than told Jim that, when Pinky walked in. I asked him if he was going to stay, and if so, Jim and I were going to lunch. I also asked Pinky if I could use his Jeep again in the morning. I told him that Jake wanted to take me to the holy part of the mountain. Pinky replied, "Of course."

Jim asked me what it was like at the sacred place Jake took me. I replied that Jake talks a lot about the Ute people's history and background. I also told Jim that I felt Jake was one of the most intelligent and fascinating people I had ever met. With that answer, I started toward the door. Waving at Pinky, I walked out with Jim right behind me. I told Pinky we would probably be back in about 30 minutes.

As Jim and I walked into Merna's, again a silence came over the place. Vonna seated us and brought over two large glasses of water. She asked if I had found out any more about the man she shot for assaulting her.

Looking at Vonna with a smile, I commented that after one of my deputies required a pillow to sit on for several days, I dropped it. Then, with somewhat of a more serious tone, I asked her if the person was bothering her anymore. She replied very quickly, "Oh no, not at all."

Vonna then asked for our order. Jim replied without hesitation that he wanted the fried chicken special, which also came with dessert. Jim asked what the dessert was and Vonna told him it was cherry pie. Jim told her that he wanted some ice cream on his pie. Winking at me, Vonna responded, "Sure thing Jim. You must have caught the sweet tooth from your boss there."

As Jim and I ate our lunch, I couldn't help but notice how much calmer he was. He was still a man of few words, not much for the small talk. By this time, the silence in Merna's was broken and people weren't staring. I think this gradual acceptance, which Jim was undoubtedly feeling, was good for him. Before leaving, I made certain to put a nice tip on the table for Vonna.

When we arrived back at the office, Pinky was ready to go. Jim told Pinky that Merna's fried chicken was really good. Pinky replied that he was going home for lunch. Thinking back, I remembered I had taken Pinky to lunch at Merna's once before the shooting incident at Vonna's. I don't think Pinky had been back since.

After a few hours, Jim asked me if he could leave early, as he wanted to help his brother fix his roof. I told him, "Sure Jim, I will see you Monday. Have a good weekend."

The remainder of the day was quiet. I was anxious to make my trip with Jake the following morning and was thinking about the upcoming Council meeting. At this meeting, the owners of the two businesses, the factory-built homes and the auto restoration shop, were going to make their case to the Council for locating on the reservation. I also expected to hear from Mr. Beaver about how he interpreted the volumes I left with him. Yes, big things ahead.

Chapter 8

"New Revelations"

The evening before my second trip with Jake to the Great Warrior, I watched the weather report. The weatherman said there would be a chill in the air in the morning. I decided it would be wise to pack a lightweight jacket for myself and Jake as well. Then I remembered, Jake was never seen without his signature blanket. It appeared as though he owned one in every color of rainbow. I found myself wondering what color blanket he'd be wearing tomorrow.

The following morning the sky was dressed in azure blue without a cloud in sight. The weatherman was right, there was a chill in the air, but it felt refreshing. The light jacket was just right.

I was happy to find Pinky's Jeep sitting in front of the office. When I walked in the door, Pinky tossed me the keys. I asked him if he needed a ride home. He told me that his wife's brother was picking him up.

Glancing out the window, I could see Jake was ready. He was draped in a vibrant orange blanket. Waving at Pinky and thanking him for the use of the Jeep, I started out the front door.

When I picked up Jake, I commented on what a beautiful morning it was. Jake replied that once again the Great Spirit was gracing us with a perfect day. As we started, I told Jake that I still needed his directions. With a smile, Jake told me to really listen this time, instead of just hearing what he said and reacting.

And listen I did. It wasn't long before we had arrived again to the sacred place. The bird's song being the only sound to break the quiet of the morning.

Jake suggested we take a walk. After several minutes Jake spoke, saying, "You know Robert, you and I, right now are taking the next step of our being." I am sure by the somewhat puzzled look on my face, Jake knew I didn't understand. With a smile Jake continued telling me that my being didn't start some 50 plus years ago, when I was born. "No," Jake said, "your being has been here since the beginning. Unless of course, Robert, you think there was a time when you did not reflect your creator. If that were to be so, then there would have been a time when your creator did not exist."

I remained speechless as Jake continued. "You were not here in your present physical form. None of us were. As a matter of fact, none of us know what forms we have taken on our journeys that brought us to this point. I suppose we took on whatever forms would help us advance most rapidly. Your spiritual form, or your being, Robert, has never changed. However, it has advanced and is continuing to advance. That's what I meant when I said that you and I were taking the next step of our being. Whether you realize it or not, your whole life up to this point has been leading you directly to this time and place. Today, you will become more aware of your spiritual path in life. You may gain more knowledge of who you really are why you are here at this point in time."

Jake then announced it was time for lunch. We walked back to the jeep and grabbed our lunch and a blanket to sit on. Jake told me that I should entertain my thoughts carefully, as the grounds where I was standing were sacred. We were in the midst of the burial grounds. Jake motioned for me to follow him and led me over to the side of the mountain.

When we reached the ledge, a strong gust of wind blew up from below and made me feel a bit off balance. Jake turned to me and said, "This is the spot. Let's spread the blanket out here." There was a beautiful view of the reservation. I could see all the way to the town of Cortez and beyond. I found myself even trying to imagine where my house was. My train of thought was interrupted by Jake's gentle voice. Jake said that we should have lunch. "I think better on a full stomach," he said with a smile.

I handed Jake one of my wife's now famous chicken salad sandwiches, followed by a now equally as famous peanut butter bar. I noticed Jake watching my left arm. Jake asked me if I thought God had changed. After looking at him for a few seconds and trying to figure out what he meant, I replied, "No." He then asked me if I thought God was different today than yesterday. Again, I replied, "No."

Pausing to take a sip of water, Jake said, "You are right. God is the same today as he was yesterday. He is the same today as he was in the beginning." And again, I replied, "Yes."

Looking again at my left arm, Jake asked me if I thought it was possible for God's reflection to change, since God hadn't. I looked at him, speechless, as I again was trying to figure out what he was saying. He then asked me if I thought people were created in the image and likeness of God. I replied, "I suppose so." He asked me if I thought the image and likeness was the same as a reflection of something. I again replied, "I suppose so."

Jake then asked, "If God hadn't changed and God's reflection hadn't changed, and if people were God's reflection, how then could people change?" And again, I replied that I guess people couldn't change either. Jake then asked me if I thought I was reflecting God any different now than I was before the accident, which left me with limited use of my left arm and leg. I didn't answer. Jake continued, "If God is the same today as God was yesterday, then God's reflection must be also. Looking at me, he said, "Right, Robert?" I replied, "Well, I guess so." He then said very firmly and directly, "If you become conscious of this really deeply and completely for a single instant, you would regain complete use of your left arm and leg."

Continuing to look at me, Jake asked, "What do you think Jesus meant when he said, 'Ye shall know the truth and the truth shall make you free?' Do you think the truth is that you reflect God? If so, Robert, then you reflect a perfect being, free of pain and sickness." Then, with a smile on his face for the first time since he had gotten on this subject, he told me to think upon these things.

Jake seemed to be enjoying the view. He broke the silence asking me if there were any more peanut butter bars. "Yes, Jake, I replied. "There's one left for you."

As I handed Jake his second peanut butter bar, he said, "Robert, sometimes what leads us toward our destiny is mysterious or can even be something we're bitter about at the time. When something spiritual is operating within our lives always take coincidences seriously and try to understand what they really mean." Continuing, Jake told me that if I could learn more about my personal mission in life, it would help me accomplish it. He then looked at me and paid me a compliment. He said that he had watched how I dealt with other people, especially my deputies and Jim. He said I seemed intent on finding the good in them. Jake then said, "Robert, whether you realize it or not, when you try to find the good in people, you are experiencing an energy within yourself, which the other people feel. This is a gift you possess, a gift brought about by those coincidences I talked about. It is actually a spiritual frequency, which you have tuned into."

Jake certainly made me feel good, but I knew I would be thinking on these concepts for a long time. I really felt as though I needed a pen and notepad when I was with Jake, because so much of what he said, I felt I forgot. At least, I thought I forgot it, as sometimes one of his statements would suddenly come into my thoughts out of the blue. Jake continued telling me that my goal in this life should be to try to understand what is happening around me. "Whether we are aware of it or not, we are all interacting spiritually with others. You have listened to your intuition and acted upon it. Your intuition is your guardian angel. "Angels, Jake explained, "are not material beings with wings, no more than God is a human or of material form." Quite the contrary, Robert. God is spiritual and sends angels to us in the form of guiding thoughts. God is the source of all these good ideas. "And, he explained, "what you feel when you entertain these protective spiritual thoughts is 'Immanuel,' or 'God with us.'" Jake went on, "Sometimes an angel thought will come to you out of nowhere. As soon as you act upon it, you can see where you were blessed by taking that course of action. God being spirit, communicates with us spiritually. Try to become aware that it is a spiritual dimension we live in. The physical part of that dimension only enables us to grow in our understanding and rise higher to new spiritual frontiers."

Jake leaned back onto the blanket and seemed to be falling asleep. I, too, leaned back and looked up at the sky, thinking on all that Jake had said. We must have drifted off to sleep.

Jake gently shook me awake saying, "It's time for us to return." Now, if you really listened to my directions on the way here, you can get us back by yourself, can't you?" And I said, "Yes," thinking in my own mind, "I hope so."

I always regretted when these excursions with Jake came to an end. So much of what he had to say always made me feel energized and happy to be alive. As I drove the Jeep toward town, I felt very much at peace and relaxed. I glanced over at Jake who had suddenly become very quiet and noticed that his eyes were closed. But I sensed by the peaceful smile on his face, he was not sleeping but meditating. I didn't feel like interrupting him.

As I drove back to town, I did remember where to turn and how far to go each way. I stopped in front of Suma's Hardware where Jake's chair was waiting. His eyes opened as soon as I stopped. As Jake reached for the door handle, he turned to me and said, "I knew you would find your way. Robert, remember what we talked about today." As Jake walked to his chair, he turned and looked at me with a smile.

As it turned out, I got back just in time, as Paul was just arriving, and I knew Pinky would need his Jeep. Much to my surprise, when I walked into the office, I found it very neat and clean. Jim was sitting in a chair near my desk. He had on a nice shirt and blue jeans, and I thought I detected something pleasant smelling, like an after shave.

As I sat down, I told Jim the coffee sure smelled good. I refrained from telling him he did too. Jim turned toward me and said he had just made a fresh pot and asked if I wanted a cup. I took Jim up on his offer. I didn't even need to tell him cream and sugar, he remembered from our lunch at Merna's.

As I drank my coffee, Jim mentioned he would sure like to get some shirts like Pinky and Paul were wearing, referring to their uniform shirts. I told him I could make that happen.

As I got in my car and started home, I couldn't help but notice how at peace I felt about leaving Jim with my deputies. I could hardly believe how they all had accepted each other. Giving Jim this job had really solved a lot of problems, for both

Jim and us. I could see Jim was taking some pride in himself. Most importantly, I hadn't smelled any alcohol on him the past several times I had talked to him. I decided to stop by Brick's and see about some uniform shirts for him. The size would be easy to pick - extra, extra-large. As it turned out, there were only four extra-extra-large uniform shirts left. I took all four.

Chapter 9

"Rich Rewards"

When I returned home from my day with Jake, my wife greeted me with good news. Mr. Beaver had called and said there had been a rather remarkable discovery regarding the matter with the Bureau of Indian Affairs.

I was so anxious to hear the news, I didn't want to wait until the next day before seeing Mr. Beaver. I didn't bother to call since it was still before closing hours. I invited Belinda to join me, telling her we'd have a nice dinner out afterwards.

Fortunately, they didn't appear to be too busy as there was no one in the reception room. Mr. Beaver walked out of his office, approaching us with a smile on his face. As I stood up to shake his hand, I remembered something Jake had said. He told me that good results would come from good intentions, especially if those intentions were unselfish and for the benefit of all. After shaking hands with Mr. Beaver, I introduced my wife. Commenting on what a pretty wife I had, Mr. Beaver invited us into his office.

Mr. Beaver handed me a document. He said it was a copy of Mr. Townsend's response from the home office of the Bureau of Indian Affairs in Washington, D.C. It stated that our government should have obtained permission from the Ute

Mountain Council and worked out payment for the additional land that was settled and expanded in 1891.

I commented to Mr. Beaver that if I was reading the letter right it sounded almost too good to be true. Looking at me from across his desk, Mr. Beaver said, "To begin with, Robert, the federal government should have bought this additional land back in 1891." He continued saying, "We are talking about thousands of acres here. I've been mulling this over ever since I received Mr. Townsend's correspondence. The land would have been worth four or five million dollars back then, not to mention what it would be worth today." Even if the Ute Mountain Indians accepted four million for the land, once you factor in the interest they would have earned, the value is out of sight.

Mr. Beaver then explained he tried to come up with a realistic figure that would have a chance of being accepted. He said there was no way we could ask for a figure that would include all the interest earnings since 1891. At this point, he commented we were looking at over 100 years. He said that four million would have easily tripled in a century and should have gone up once again for the last quarter. He said the figure he had in mind was 16 million. He also said that the government was prepared to settle for this figure.

"At 16 million," Mr. Beaver continued, "we would be looking at a figure near what the land would be worth today. Still below, he added, but an amount we stand a good chance of getting." I wondered how much his fee for this would be. Like he had read my mind, he said, "Since I've worked on this for a few weeks, I'm prepared to settle for a quarter of a million."

My wife and I sat there speechless. After a long silence, he finally spoke up and asked me to take this information and his offer to the Council and let him know when a decision had been made. I stood up walked toward Mr. Beaver's desk saying,

"Excuse me for being temporarily speechless." I'm somewhat overwhelmed." I knew I had tears in my eyes. I continued telling him how grateful I was for his efforts. I also told him I thought his fee was more than fair. I said I was going to get in touch with the Council this evening and asked him if he would be available to accompany me to a Council meeting next Monday evening at 7:00 p.m. I offered to come by and pick him up. He took me up on my offer.

After Belinda and I dined at a local restaurant that served delicious Mexican food, we returned home. Most of our dinner conversation revolved around what we had just learned from Mr. Beaver. I knew I wouldn't be able to wait to tell at least one Council member the amazing news, so I called Truman as soon as I got home. I apologized for calling him at home, but I had a feeling he'd be glad I did. I told him I had the most amazing news to share at Monday's Council meeting.

After relating all that Mr. Beaver had shared with me, Truman's joy almost surpassed my own. I then suggested what Jake had brought to my attention when he first learned of what I was pursuing - that each person on the reservation would receive an initial payment, somewhere around $20,000 each, and then receive the balance in monthly payments over the next 20 years.

I told Truman, that with the current stock market, it was not the best time for the residents to risk their finances. I further explained that receiving a large amount of money such as several hundred thousand dollars, might be overwhelming and could end up being wasted.

Truman liked my suggestion and asked if I would explain my thoughts to the Council. I said absolutely. I don't know why but I was hit with something Jake had said about controlling situations through spiritual love and how we handled an event depended on the path we had taken thus far. If Jake was right, and the coincidences I had experienced so far in life had brought me to this particular time and place, I wanted to understand more about them so I wouldn't make any mistakes.

When I fell asleep that night, I had no dreams. I didn't toss and turn, nor wake up in the night, but rather had one of the most restful night's sleeps I could ever remember.

When I awoke in the morning, even though it was one of my days off, I told Belinda after breakfast that I wanted to go to the reservation for a while. I know my inner thoughts were guiding me out to visit with Jake.

As I pulled into town, I looked towards Jake's chair to see if he was there. I was afraid because of the chill in the air he might not be there, but there he sat. As I walked up to Jake, I asked him if he would like to sit in my car and visit for a while. He smiled, but said, "No, I'm fine here," he said as he pulled a pearl white blanket tighter around his shoulders. I stood there for a moment, trying to find where to begin.

Jake could see I was struggling, so he asked me what good news I had today. Once again, almost feeling as if Jake could read my mind, I asked him how he knew the news was good. Jake replied with a smile, "When you are looking for good news, you usually find it." Motioning to a chair close by, Jake invited me to sit with him.

After sitting down and scooting my chair closer to his, I told Jake the same good news I had told Truman. I also told Jake I was going to take his advice and recommend to the Council the payments be made to the residents in monthly installments.

At the end of my explanation, Jake told me that he could tell by my enthusiasm and diligence that I had given this matter some serious thought. Jake then leaned his head back and closed his eyes. I knew that he was neither resting nor ignoring me. No, I knew Jake was getting ready to come up with some words to inspire me, which I needed.

Opening his eyes and turning toward me, he said, "Robert, once again you are witnessing love in operation. Because of your sincere, unselfish concern for others, certain events in your life, which some would call 'coincidences', have you led you to this point. Fortunately for my people, it sounds like they're going to profit from it. Something spiritual is operating everywhere, Robert. I know we are all aware of the material, or what we see, but this is really a spiritual universe we live in. It is merely our five physical senses that suggest otherwise."

Changing to a serious look, Jake said, "If you try to control any situations that might arise at the Council meeting, do it with spiritual love. Remember, Robert, your whole life and the road you have traveled have led you directly to this point. Just look back at all your experiences and decisions that brought you to this moment, at this time."

Glancing toward the office, I saw Pinky walking in the front door. I told Jake I was happy I had the chance to talk, but I should check on Pinky and see how things were going.

As I walked in the front door of the office, I found Pinky and Jim both sitting at Pinky's desk having a cup of coffee. I greeted them both and asked how things were going. Pinky commented that things were going fine. I couldn't help but notice, as I glanced around the office, how organized everything looked.

I told Jim I'd ordered four uniform shirts for him, and I would pick them up Monday morning on my way to work. He looked at me with gratitude and uttered a soft, "thank you."

As I walked back outside, I couldn't help but notice how much colder it was getting. Looking over toward Jake's chair, I noticed Jake also had a blanket wrapped around his legs. I waved at him again as I stepped down off the porch and headed toward my car. I felt much better about the upcoming Council meeting after talking to Jake.

Monday morning arrived with a chill in the air. After picking up Jim's uniform shirts at Brick's I headed to Towaoc.

Back in town, I saw Jake walk up to his chair and sit down with a dark navy blanket around his shoulders. I immediately left the office and headed in his direction

Before I could say a word Jake asked if today was the day of the special Council meeting. I told him it was, and I was hoping they would make the right decision regarding how much money to seek, and more importantly, how to receive the payments. Looking at me seriously, Jake said, "Robert, try to take all of your preconceived notions about this matter out of your mind, if you can, and try to imagine or know that the Council will make the right decision. If our pathways in life, I mean yours, mine, and the Council members, have brought us to this point to make this decision, then the right decision will be made."

I had been feeling nervous, but after listening to Jake, I felt completely at ease. Glancing over at the office, I saw Jim standing on the porch, looking in our direction. He had on his new uniform shirt. Looking back at Jake, I told him I would spend the rest of the day knowing the matter would be resolved for the betterment of all. I thanked Jake for his thoughts and headed toward Jim.

As I arrived on the front porch, Jim gave me a smile and said he thought the shirt fit well and asked me what I thought. I said, "You look great! Like an official member of the team."

The rest of the day went by fast. I went home, ate dinner, and after kissing my wife goodbye I was off to pick up Mr. Beaver. I arrived at Mr. Beaver's at 6:30 p.m. After he had introduced me to his wife, we started for my car. It was still chilly out, but it was a clear and beautiful evening.

After turning onto the highway and nearing the reservation, Mr. Beaver told me that he had lived here for over 30 years, and this was the first time he had ever seen the reservation. He also said he had never actually thought of how the Sleeping Ute Mountain really did resemble an American Indian lying on his back. This evening the colors were spectacular. A soft green haze covered the whole Ute Mountain range. The sun was just setting in a lavender blue sky. It was a beautiful sight to see.

Upon arriving at the Council building, we were met by Truman. After I introduced them to each other, Mr. Beaver commented that the new building was certainly impressive. I could tell that made Truman feel good. As we entered the Council chambers, I could see all the Council members were there. A silence had fallen over the room. Turning to Truman, I asked him to please introduce the Council members to Mr. Beaver, as I wasn't even sure I knew everyone's names yet. As Truman introduced each member, Mr. Beaver seemed very much at ease, reaching out and shaking hands with each Council member. Truman announced Mr. Beaver and I had the floor.

Mr. Beaver asked if I would help pass out some documents. As I did, Mr. Beaver told the Council members that he would give them time to look over the information, but that it was mostly guidelines for them to utilize as he discussed the various payment disbursement alternatives.

Mr. Beaver began by telling the Council that their Security Chief and Head of Indian Affairs, Mr. Brown, had recently brought him volumes containing some questionable agreements and treaties that their forefathers and the American government had entered into. Mr. Beaver continued telling them that after he had read these treaties, he felt that egregious errors had been made. These errors had been made over 100 years ago, and he was convinced that they were not made intentionally but rather through oversight and negligence.

Looking at me and raising his eyebrows a little, he said, "As a result, the government may owe the Ute Mountain Ute Tribe Reservation residents quite a bit of money, and rightfully so.

The government may owe the residents as much as forty million dollars for land which was developed by early settlers, land which was supposed to be a buffer zone between the reservation land and settlements outside the reservation." The Council members were all speechless. Mr. Suma spoke up first, asking Mr. Beaver to explain what land he was referring to. Mr. Beaver answered by saying he was referring to most of the land where the town of Cortez was located and many housing developments near the reservations.

Truman asked Mr. Beaver what course of action, if any, he would recommend. Mr. Beaver explained he had been in contact with Mr. Townsend at the Bureau of Indian Affairs in Washington, D.C. and had discussed the matter with him.

He explained that the forty million dollars did not include interest for the past 100 years, but he felt that if we pointed this error out to Washington, and dropped the interest owed, that a fair price to consider would be 30 million. He explained the reservation was more likely to get a settlement in that amount far quicker plus, they wouldn't have to go to court.

One of the Council members then asked Mr. Beaver what his fee would be. Mr. Beaver answered that if there could be a quick settlement that didn't involve court time, his fee would be one quarter of a million dollars. A brief silence fell over the Council, and I stood up and asked Mr. House if I might comment briefly. He agreed. I told the Council that the one quarter of a million dollars would actually be a very conservative fee to pay for Mr. Beaver's legal services. I explained further that 25% of the entire settlement is what other law firms would mostly likely charge.

One of the Council members stood up and declared that he didn't know what he would do with his share of all that money. Mr. Beaver responded saying, "Mr. Brown and I have put a pen to it and came up with a good way for the reservation residents to receive payment. We recommend giving each resident of the reservation over the age of 18 $20,000 initially, and then continue to pay them $2,000 a month for 20 years."

The whole Council broke into applause. Things got so noisy, that Mr. House couldn't hear me trying to get his attention. He finally saw me waving at him, so he called the meeting to order. I told Mr. House and the Council that if they were satisfied with Mr. Beaver asking for thirty million on their behalf, and if the type of payment he suggested was satisfactory, that someone should make a motion to allow Mr. Beaver to proceed. Mr. Suma immediately stood up and said, "I so move." After one of the other members seconded his motion, Truman called for the vote. It passed unanimously.

As the Council members continued to visit with each other, Mr. Beaver and I walked toward the door. Truman saw us and came over offering his hand to Mr. Beaver. He told Mr. Beaver how grateful they all were for his work and efforts, and they would wait to hear from him. Mr. Beaver agreed to make this his priority saying they would hear from him as soon as he had an answer.

As Mr. Beaver and I started back to his home, I asked him how he thought things went. Turning to me, and with a serious tone, he said he was somewhat surprised. He said he hadn't expected a meeting to be conducted that orderly. He said he had handled numerous cases involving large settlement amounts before, and not a one had such a harmonious outcome. He said this was extraordinarily rare.

As I arrived in front of Mr. Beaver's home, I thanked him and told him it was a good thing we were doing. Turning to me as he got out, he said he hadn't felt so good in a long time, and it's not just because of the generous fee he was going to receive, it was the fact that this would positively impact the reservation for generations. He assured me we wouldn't have any trouble at all reaching a fair and generous settlement.

After arriving home, I found Belinda waiting up for me. By this time, she had also become emotionally invested in the outcome. She wanted to know how the issue had been resolved. I told her how well everything had transpired and of Mr. Beaver's confidence in reaching the right settlement with the officials in Washington.

After chatting a while, we retired for the evening. As I was lying in bed, reflecting on the meeting, I remembered the meetings I had set up for Monday with the local businesses regarding moving their operations onto the reservation. I also wanted to remind them about attending the upcoming Council meeting as well. I then drifted off to sleep feeling at ease with how well things were unfolding.

When I awoke the next morning, I noticed darkness was lingering a little longer. It was just barely getting light as I pulled out of the driveway and started toward to the reservation. I was eager to visit with Jake that day and talk over the outcome of the Council meeting. As I pulled over and parked behind our security office, I glanced in the direction of Jake's chair. I was disappointed to find it empty. As I walked in the front door and looked in Jay's direction, he said, "You've got company." I immediately looked toward my desk, and to my surprise, there sat Jake, a warm brown blanket around his shoulders.

Glancing over to the coffee pot, I saw it was about half full. Jim had arrived and left a box of donuts in the table. Turning to Jake, I told him what a pleasant surprise it was to see him, and I wanted to talk to him. I offered him some coffee and a donut. Jake replied that just a donut would be nice. Jay got up from his desk about that time and told me he was heading out and bid Jake and I farewell.

After I had poured myself a cup of coffee and took a donut, I joined Jake. He said that he had been thinking all week about the Council meeting. He continued that when he got up this morning and looked out his window at the Great Warrior, it appeared as if the mountain was covered with a field of sacred energy. Jake said that he sensed from this that something of significance was either happening now or was about to happen.

I told him the Council meeting went very well and all the Council members seemed to like Mr. Beaver. I informed Jake of everything that happened at the meeting, including the recommendation of how to receive payment.

Jake sat back in his chair with a look of utter contentment. He told me he knew I had put a lot of my attention into this matter, and that he had found so far in his life's experiences that where your attention and desires dwell is where your life's energy flows. "I think you know by now Robert, "I'm not talking about your physical energy, I'm talking about your spiritual energy. It is our spiritual energy that supplies us with the right thoughts and ideas."

After finishing his donut, Jake got up and walked toward the front door. Turning and looking back at me, he said, "Before the cold weather sets in, we will have to make another journey to visit with the Great Warrior."

I told Jake to just let me know when and I would have Belinda fix us a lunch. Jake told me that he would like to meet her. I told him that the next time I brought her out to the reservation, I would see that he got to.

After Jake left, I dove into what I needed to accomplish that day. I contacted Mr. Brooks, owner of the auto restoration shop in Durango, and Mr. Moriarty, who runs the factory-built homes business. I asked them both to fax me some copies of their plans for expansion on the reservation. I then headed out to scout locations on the reservation that might work for them. I decided for the next month, assuming all went well, and no big security problems came up, I would concentrate all my efforts on finding suitable locations for the two businesses.

I needed Truman to help me find out just how many of the local people would be interested in learning new trades and would seek employment. I also was interested in learning how many might have experience in either field. Of course, we would need to coordinate with the business owners regarding offering the proper training for their potential employees.

Just thinking about the possibility of a large government settlement and hundreds of residents gaining employment on the reservation, gave me a tremendous sense of fulfillment and joy.

In the next few days, my three deputies kept things running smoothly. I still had to marvel over how well Jim was getting along with everyone. I think their friendship had even spilled over to off duty hours. I know Bill sure had a smile on his face these days, waving at Jim and I whenever he saw us strolling over to Merna's for a quick lunch.

The day of the Council meeting had arrived. The owners of the factory-built home business and the auto restoration shop made effective presentations at the meeting. They both, however, wanted to see some possible sites, or even some abandoned buildings that might be converted to fit their needs. They were onboard to set up training classes for residents who were interested. Between Truman and I, we had found six possible sites. We hadn't considered converting some existing buildings into factories, which would certainly be a more affordable route to go.

Mr. Beaver's office contacted me during the first week of November. I was surprised to hear from them so soon, as it had only been two weeks since our meeting with the Council. Mr. Beaver's secretary asked me if it would be possible for me to come by their office on my way home from work, as Mr. Beaver had some very good news for me.

After hearing her mention "very good news," I knew that I would be much too excited to wait. I told her I would rather come right over if Mr. Beaver had time to see me. After checking with Mr. Beaver, she told me to come on in.

When I arrived at Mr. Beaver's office, he met me with a big smile on his face and told me I had better sit down. Mr. Beaver explained that he didn't even get a chance to tell Mr. Townsend the amount the Council had given him the authority to ask for. Barely able to contain his excitement, Mr. Beaver burst out saying, "The government is offering a sixty-million-dollar settlement!"

Barely able to talk through his ear-to-ear grin, Mr. Beaver said this means that instead of $20,000 initially per resident, it would be $40,000, and instead of $2,000 a month for the next 20 years, each resident would now receive $3,000 a month. I was jubilant. At this point, I told Mr. Beaver that I knew the figure he had given to the Council for his services, but that I felt since his efforts resulted in twice as much as they were expecting, that his fee should also be doubled. He enthusiastically replied, "No objection, your honor!" I couldn't wait to get back to the office.

As soon as I arrived, I called Truman with the good news. I quickly ran the government's offer by him, and he was also beyond overjoyed. I told Truman I felt a special Council meeting was more than justified for tomorrow evening. He agreed and said that after Mr. Beaver talked to the Council, he would call a tribal meeting of all the reservation residents. It would be up to him and the rest of the Council members to explain everything to the residents. He told me that I might not want to stay for that meeting, as it may go on all night. He was sure there would be much celebrating after the meeting. I also told Truman about my latest thoughts concerning Mr. Beaver's fee. Truman agreed, saying he felt the Council would feel the same way. At any rate, he would certainly bring the matter up at the meeting.

The following evening, I picked up Mr. Beaver and we headed for the meeting. The weather had turned cold, and it was dark when Mr. Beaver and I arrived. Earlier that day, I had called my three deputies and told them that the tribal meeting following the special Council meeting was very important, and that I wanted all of them to attend and represent the security department. I said I would relieve Paul so they all could attend.

Mr. Beaver handled the Council meeting masterfully. He patiently answered all questions concerning how much each resident would receive, and when the payments would start. I figured Mr. Beaver's right hand as well as his back must have been getting a little sore, as every time I looked at him, he was getting a handshake and a pat on the back. Truman also told Mr. Beaver he had talked to the Council members, and they unanimously agreed to double his legal fee.

After dropping Mr. Beaver at his house and thanking him again for all he had done, I headed back into to town to relieve Paul so he could join his fellow residents at the tribal meeting.

Truman was right. The gathering did go all night. My three deputies stopped in the office around midnight looking beyond happy. Pinky said now they knew what I had been up to running back and forth to town and spending so much time with Truman. Jay, looking at me with an exaggerated seriousness said he may not be in for work anymore, that he was going to retire now that he was rich. He then winked at me, chuckling, saying with five children at home, he wouldn't be retiring any time soon.

The next morning, just before Pinky arrived, Jim came in with not one, but two boxes of donuts. As he went to make coffee, I told Jim not to bother, since I'd been there all night, I had kept the coffee maker busy and a fresh pot was waiting for him. Looking at me and talking in Jim's soft-spoken way, he said, "With the good you've done for Towaoc, I may have to take me a wife, Brown." Pinky walked in about that time. I told both Pinky and Jim about the other news regarding locating two factories on the reservation. Pinky, laughing, said I had better keep those donuts coming or he may want to try his hand at auto painting.

I responded that I'd seen Pinky's penmanship, he'd better stick to being a deputy. I then bid a smiling Jim and Pinky farewell. As is my habit, I glanced over toward Jake's chair. There he sat in all his splendor. Today he was wrapped in a dark red blanket. He motioned for me to come over.

Jake commented that yesterday had been a great day. I nodded in agreement. Pointing up toward the Sleeping Ute Mountain, Jake commented that the early American Indians thought there was treasure upon the knees of the Great Warrior. Turning to me, he said, "You know, Robert, we found that treasure yesterday."

I was more than ready for Jake's timely wisdom, so I pulled up a chair next to him and scooted in close. Looking again toward the Sleeping Ute, Jake said that the real treasure to be found is our true spiritual selfhood. Turning and looking at me intently, he said, "I feel as if you have found some of your true spiritual selfhood, Robert. You were able to do this by quieting your five physical senses and listening to your innermost thoughts the past few months." He continued saying many mysterious events had guided me to the reservation, and what I was experiencing was in fact, my destiny for this phase of life. Jake continued saying that caring about my fellowmen helped link me to God and connect me with my destiny. "You see Robert, "When you become unconcerned, you become disconnected."

Then, Jake said, "Robert, you are evolving into a higher state of energy. I want you to understand that this new state of energy and spiritual inspiration can manifest in unexpected ways." Jake could tell by the look on my face that I was a bit bewildered by his last statement. It almost sounded as if he were saying that in order to achieve any higher in my understanding, I would have to transform my material body into a spiritual form. Of course, I only knew of one way that would happen, and it was not a pleasant thought.

Sitting back in his chair and looking in the direction of the Sleeping Ute, he said, "You know Robert, our life here on this phase of existence consists of us expanding our consciousness. When we reach a point in this life where we've gone as far as we can go, it is time to go on to the next phase. In other words, Robert, when you reach a point in your life where you can rise no higher spiritually, or you are no longer replacing your physical thoughts with spiritual ones, for your own benefit, it is best to go on to the next phase, where you can continue to advance."

Jake continued, "We all must advance in our thinking until we replace all hate with love, all regret with joy, sickness with health, sinful ways with righteousness, and finally, death with a spiritual understanding of what life is." Looking at me with his blue eyes sparkling, Jake said, "At that point, we will become as one with our Creator. Because, you see, all of those things that we are striving to become and understand are what our Creator is." With that statement, Jake became somewhat silent.

Jake, sensing my unease with this growing revelation, urged me not to worry about comprehending all he was saying right now; everything would eventually come to light.

I told Jake he had certainly given me a lot to think about and I was going home to get some rest. As I walked toward the security office, Jake called to me to be careful. I replied back, "I will, Jake."

When I got home, I had breakfast with my wife then went to our bedroom for some rest. The smell of winter was in the air, laced with the scent of fireplace smoke.

I woke up around dinnertime. I called to check in with the office, and Paul assured me that everything was fine, but he had not seen Jim all day.

Chapter 10

"Final Trial"

After dinner, my wife and I sat up visiting until almost 11:00 p.m. At that time, I told her that we should go to bed, as I wanted to get up and go in early the following morning and meet with Truman. I wanted to find out how the tribal meeting went.

We had just fallen asleep when the phone rang. When my wife picked up the phone, I could hear an agitated Paul on the line. She handed me the phone with a scared look on her face. She told me that I had better get this quick, there had been a shooting.

I took the phone. Paul was talking so fast I had to ask him to slow down and start over. Paul said the dispatcher for the Montezuma County Sheriff's Department just called and said one of our deputies had shot and killed one of their officers at Erma's Tavern in Cortez.

I asked Paul if the shooter was still there and if he knew whether it was Pinky or Jay. Paul said the dispatcher informed him the deputy in question had fled the scene and described him as a very large man. I was hit with a feeling of immense dread and suddenly felt sick to my stomach. Pinky had told me earlier that he hadn't seen Jim all day. I imagine, as much as Jim liked his uniform shirt, he probably wore it into town. I didn't want to believe it was Jim. He was doing so well.

Paul told me he could hear sirens. I told him to go to Jim's brother's house immediately, as I had a feeling that was where the sirens were headed. I told him to tell whoever was in charge that I was on my way and would be there in under 10 minutes.

As I hung up the phone, my wife was holding my shirt for me. After she helped me get my arms into it, she reached for my pants. My hands were shaking so much I couldn't button my sleeves. She also needed to help me button the front of my shirt. She even helped me put my gun belt on. My left arm couldn't even support the front of the belt so I could buckle it. As I ran for the front door, my wife was in tears saying, "You don't have any business doing this. I told you that you shouldn't do this again." Trying to get control of my voice, I assured her that I would be very careful.

As I hurried for my car, I noticed my movement was getting worse. I thought I had been doing better. It must be all the excitement that was making me unsteady. Once I started driving, I gained more control over my emotions. The dispatcher radioed me and confirmed my suspicions that the 'shooter' had headed to Jim's brother's house.

As I pulled up in front of Jim's brother's home, there were about half a dozen patrol cars parked sideways around the parameter of the house with officers poised behind them with handguns and rifles raised. I recognized this configuration from the serious disturbances I worked in Wichita. Things were not looking good.

I walked over to where the largest group was standing, thinking I'd find someone in charge. I introduced myself to an officer with captain's bars who was holding a bullhorn and asked him to brief me on what was going on. He responded by saying, "What do you mean, brief you? One of your deputies killed one of my men in cold blood." Trying to calm the captain down I gestured for him to walk over to a spot where we could share a word privately. I told him the man inside wasn't one of my deputies even though he had on a deputy shirt that said otherwise. "His name is Jim Goodriver," I explained. "He works for me doing light office work and running errands. I got him the shirt to help him feel more like a part of our team." I continued saying there was a strong possibility that another man, a woman, and two children were also in the house. I then asked for his bullhorn, saying I would be able to talk Jim into letting them leave the house.

The captain handed me bullhorn with a scornful look. I told him that I didn't want him or his men to get concerned over what I was going to say, that I was going to say whatever it took to calm the situation and for him to let me do my job. Without waiting for permission, I walked away from the group and stepped into the front yard under the streetlight so Jim could see me. Turning on the bullhorn, I told Jim there would be no shooting, and to let his brother and family come on out. I assured him that I would take care of them and not let anyone shoot. I reminded him of how good his brother's family had been to him, and how I knew he didn't want any harm to come to them.

Nothing happened for a few seconds. Then, the front porch light came on and the family appeared one by one, coming out the front door.

Jim's niece and nephew and sister-in-law were in tears. I walked them and Jim's brother over to a group of officers. Other than being visibly shaken up, they all seemed to be okay.

I then told the captain I wanted to try to persuade Jim into letting me enter the house and talk to him. I asked him to hold off from doing anything else until I at least tried, as I didn't want to see anyone else hurt.

Again, without asking for permission, I walked back into the light with the bullhorn. As I raised the bullhorn to speak to Jim, a shot rang out from inside the house. I pushed my dread aside however, as it sounded as if the shot went up into the air and hit the ceiling. I immediately raised my right hand, which was holding the bullhorn, up in the air in the direction of the officers. I yelled to them not to shoot, that I thought it was only a warning shot Jim had fired. I told Jim that he had just taken about 10 years off my life. I asked him if he would let me come in and visit with him so we could figure out what we were going to do next. Jim yelled out and told me to stay away from the house. He said that if I came any closer, he would shoot me. I replied, "Jim, my friend, you and I have come a long way together." I continued saying, "I don't know exactly what happened, but I want to hear your side. Keeping you alive is my top priority. You know you can trust me, Jim."

There was no response from Jim. The captain standing behind me with the other officers yelled, "Let us handle things now! You will just get shot."

I knew it was coming to that, as it seemed we had exhausted all other options. With that in mind, I said, "Jim, I'm taking my gun belt off and laying it on the ground here. I am afraid these guys will kill you, so I'm coming on in. I am unarmed Jim, and you know you can trust me." As I put my gun belt down, I started walking toward the house. Jim yelled louder than ever, "I'll shoot you, Brown." I had left the bullhorn lying with my gun belt, so I yelled out that I knew he wouldn't, and I was coming in.

When I reached the porch, I heard the front door unlatch. There was a cold chill in the air, and I was shaking badly, more from the fear I felt than from the temperature. I walked in to find Jim pointing a gun at me. I immediately told Jim to put the gun down and tell me exactly what had happened earlier at the tavern.

Jim started sobbing. After he gained his composure, he told me that an officer who had arrested him before for being drunk was laughing and making fun of him in his uniform. He said the officer saw that he was not wearing a gun and told him if he were really a deputy, he would have a gun. Jim said when he walked toward the door to leave, and the officer pulled out his gun and stuck it in his face. Jim said he tried to go around him, but he struck him on the side of his head with his gun. Jim then explained he threw the officer to the floor and a struggle ensued. He said he tried to grab the gun because he was afraid the officer would shoot him. While he was struggling to get the gun, it discharged shooting the officer in the chest and killing him instantly.

Jim said he ran because he knew if more officers came, they wouldn't believe him and would shoot him. I believed him and I told him I did. I also told him that if I could get him out of the house and into one of the patrol cars, I would ride in with him and see that nothing happened to him. And, if they did need to lock him up, I would stay with him.

Reaching my hand out, Jim gave me the gun. I stuck it in my rear pocket as I walked to the front door. Stepping out onto the porch, I yelled out to the officers that there had been enough violence for one night and cautioned anyone against trying to take matters into their own hands. I knew there would be some hostile feelings about this, as one of their comrades had been killed, and sometimes revenge takes over, and that would be hard to control.

I instructed Jim to walk behind me. I also told him that he would have to stoop down quite a bit, but to keep his head down behind me. I then yelled to the officers that we were coming out. We stepped off the porch and slowly started walking.

As we advanced towards the officers, a rush of wind blew in, swirling around Jim and me and scattering the officers' hats into the street. It was at this point that I recalled Jake's words of caution to me earlier that morning. When we were about halfway to the larger group of officers, a shot rang out.

Everything suddenly became very bright. My head felt warm, and my vision blurred. I collapsed in Jim's arms. I could barely make out the outline of his face as he leaned over me. Suddenly the brightness left, and everything became dark. The bullet from one of the officer's guns had entered at the side of my right eye and exited out the left side of my head. If it had gone straight through from front to back side, it would have hit Jim, too.

I was unable to speak, but with my left eye, I could see several officers converge on Jim. After getting Jim on the ground, they had to use leg irons to restrain him because the handcuffs would not fit his wrists.

By this time, an ambulance had arrived. After learning which hospital I was being taken to, the captain instructed an officer to go pick up my wife. I think he thought I was dead or would be soon.

They put Jim in a patrol car. I recalled how he hated being confined. However, Jim wasn't resisting. He was just staring coldly straight ahead.

When the ambulance pulled up in front of the emergency room, a team of doctors were waiting. The paramedic told them I had a very weak pulse and was in shock. The attending physician, Dr. Connolly, advised the staff I would need a neurosurgeon. The closest one was in Durango, some 60 miles away. One of the officers standing by said they could get the neurosurgeon a police escort or maybe even a helicopter to get them here faster.

By this time, the officer had arrived with my wife. She was weeping and visibly upset. Belinda was asked to sign papers giving the physicians authority to act in my best interest. My wife was then ushered into the waiting room where a chaplain had been waiting to offer support and comfort.

After about an hour had passed, the neurosurgeon arrived. Shortly after his arrival, the attending physician entered the waiting room and asked to speak to my wife. He told her I had lost a lot of blood and due to the extent of the injury there was nothing they could do. He said they would do all they could to make sure I didn't experience any pain. Belinda took the news hard, asking the chaplain if he could call our children, as she wasn't up to it.

During everything, I was awake and could see through my left eye, however I was unable to speak. The words were in my head, but they wouldn't make it to my mouth.

About this time, Truman and several Council members had arrived. Accompanying them were my three deputies. My wife had never met them, and I think they were a comfort to her. My wife knowing how much Jake meant to me, asked Truman to have one of the Council members to bring him to the hospital.

I could tell by their discussions that the officer who fired the shot had strong ties with the officer who had been accidentally killed by Jim. He knew the officer's family and he let his emotions overrule his better judgment. He thought he had a clear shot at Jim. I know he was devastated that he had shot me instead.

I understood how officers' emotions could affect their duty and their work. It was the human side of them coming out and they had feelings like everyone else. It would be nice if an officer could put their emotions in a box when they were on duty and then take them out when they were done. But it didn't work that way.

Dr. Connolly came into the waiting room again and told my wife they were placing me in a room in the west wing, facing the Sleeping Ute. It was about 6:00 in the morning and many of the reservation residents had gathered on the lawn outside my window.

The county officers had been updated on my condition. Jim overheard their conversation from his cell and asked to speak to someone of authority, or possibly the County Sheriff. He was insisting for permission to come and see me. By this time, the sheriff and the county officers had interviewed several witnesses and learned the truth about the incident at the Tavern. They now knew Jim had only acted in his own self-defense. And because he had been calm and cooperative, the deputies agreed.

It was now about 6:00 in the morning. The heart monitor showed that my heart was growing weaker. When Jim arrived, he stopped just short of coming into the room. He had a deputy on each side of him. My wife, Truman, Pinky, Paul, and Jay were all in my room. As Jim stepped in, Truman introduced him to my wife. My wife, who had been sitting down beside me, got up and went over and embraced him.

Jim walked over to my bedside and looked down on me. A tear escaped him and fell lightly on my cheek, and he reached out and squeezed my hand. Even through the heavy pain medication coursing through my veins, I winced a bit. Jim really was a gentle giant; he had no idea how incredibly strong he was.

Truman asked my wife if he could open the curtains covering the large window in my room. He wanted the residents gathering outside to know which room I was in. My wife agreed and he pulled them open, waving to the residents below. The group below then broke into a rhythmic chant. Truman said they were dressed in Native costume and were dancing and praying to the Great Spirit.

As if on cue, Jake entered my room bringing with him a blast of air. Through my one good eye, I could see his blanket displayed every color of the rainbow. Truman introduced him to Belinda. Jake embraced my wife warmly, never taking his gaze from me. He indicated for Truman to come over to where he was and look at me. Then he pointed out the window toward the Sleeping Ute. Truman's mouth opened wide. I was lying in the same position, mirroring the Great Warrior, on my back with one arm folded over my chest, and my knee slightly raised. It had snowed during the night in the high country, covering the Sleeping Ute in a blanket of white, resembling the white sheet pulled over me.

Jake came over to my beside and put his hand on my shoulder. Then he bent down and whispered softly, "You've done good, Robert. The good have done, is the good you are, and it is the good you will take with you. You are ready to begin your next big adventure." He then kissed me on the check, saying "Godspeed, great warrior, Godspeed."

Then the heart monitor stopped. One of the physicians came over and checked my pulse. Then he turned off the heart monitor and pulled the sheet over my head, releasing the sheet in a way that it resembled the Sleeping Ute's head feather.

The chaplain put his arm around my wife and led her out of the room. Truman, with his head down, followed. Pinky, Paul, and Jay asked Jim to accompany them back to the jail. Jake was the last one to leave.

Chapter 11

"Spiritual Phase"

I felt free and light all at once, basking in a sense of peace and tranquility I had never felt before. It is as if a great sense of love had taken control of my whole being. I wasn't even capable of thinking an unkind thought. I sensed people leaving my room and I could hear their tears, but I didn't feel sadness or loss. I was only filled with feelings of love and compassion.

I felt as if I was being sustained by another source of energy. And this energy was comprised of love, happiness, peace, and the embodiment of good. Jake said when I experience these feelings of total love, I will become one with my Creator. I have now learned that my Creator is love.

I felt genuine love for everyone, including the officer who shot me. I felt embraced in the arms of love. I am happiness. I am harmony. I am bliss.

As Jake expressed it, this new phase takes place beyond physical boundaries, existing in a spiritual realm, where spiritual senses have taken the place of my five physical ones. I was thinking about Jake and trying to envision where he was, and I found myself transported to where he was walking down the hospital hall. Although I was just there in thought, Jake must have felt my presence, as he turned around and gave me a knowing smile and a wave goodbye. It was then I knew, this great man walked between worlds, and was indeed a holy man. He was sent to me to be my spirit guide and he had done his job extraordinarily well.

I was aware I was leaving the only world I'd known, where I relied on the five physical senses to define my existence. I was becoming one with my Source, being anywhere and everywhere that source is. I knew I was going to have to learn how to navigate this new spiritual phase, but I also knew Jake had given me a strong start. I now understood what Jake was referring to when he said love and compassion is what matters and is where my true strength lies. Surrounded by love, there is no room for disharmony; all is love. Where I am is not a place. I dwell in an inner sense of peace. Jake told me I was as real as my source, that I was the same as my source by reflection. I understand now that my source is God.

I was elated to be shed of the limitations of my physical body and my ungraceful movements. I was perfect and whole. I was not the least bit tired. I don't know if I will ever sleep again.

On this new spiritual phase of existence, I am the embodiment of happiness and contentment, emanating from a Divine source. I think we all emanate from this Divine source. If we're all thoughts from this source, then we are all one with the source. Since all I am now are feelings, I know that here where I am, in this realm of complete happiness, we are all one. We are all exactly alike, experiencing the same feelings of love.

I wouldn't trade this new existence for anything I experienced on the physical phase. I am not leaving anything, but instead I'm going on and rising higher. I don't know if there will be more phases to achieve or not, but I am quite happy in this one. I can't really find the words to describe in a human language, where I am. There are no physical forms here. I have not experienced any darkness, only light. This place is filled with total happiness and serenity. I don't feel sickness, pain, or sorrow. There will be no sin. I don't really know what those feelings are anymore.

I believe that my life reflects my Creator, my source. In fact, I understand now that it always has, I was just not aware of it. I may have been on other phases of existence prior to this last one, but I hope there isn't any beyond this.

I also believe that every one of you will eventually arrive on this absolute phase. You will experience the same joyous feelings I am experiencing, knowing nothing but genuine love. Because love is all there really is. I am just one continuous thought: a soul without end, in a world without end.

Because I could everywhere all at once, I could see the Council members had joined the reservation residents on the lawn. Jake, Jim, and my deputies were leaving from the front doors of the hospital. After arriving at the bottom of the steps, a gust of wind blew in and danced around Jake and Jim almost playfully before moving past them. I knew at that moment, Jake had found a new student. Jake stopped Jim and pointed toward the Sleeping Ute, saying "The Great Warrior is at peace now." By this time, the rising sun had started to melt the snow blanketing the Ute Mountains, revealing the Great Warrior in all his glory.

> Through faith we understand that the worlds were framed by the word of God, so that things which are seen were not made of things which do appear.
>
> —Hebrews 11:3

EPILOGUE

Jim was eventually released from the county jail, as the investigation exonerated him, proving the shooting was accidental and brought about by the officer who was killed.

Jake still occupies his chair almost daily, weather permitting, on the south wall of the hardware store keeping a watchful eye on the Great Warrior and the residents of Towaoc.

Jim went back to helping Pinky and Paul at the security office. Jay, even with five children, was able to retire. Eventually, Jim received a deputy's commission from the Montezuma County Sheriff. He, Pinky and Paul made quite a team. Jim eventually married one of the women who had grown up on the reservation. They had a son. They named him Robert.

www.ingramcontent.com/pod-product-compliance
Lightning Source LLC
Chambersburg PA
CBHW071007120626
46546CB00003B/977